Ethical Perspectives on Business and Society

Ethical Perspectives on Business and Society

Edited by

Yerachmiel Kugel
Gladys W. Gruenberg
Saint Louis University

Lexington Books
D.C. Heath and Company
Lexington, Massachusetts
Toronto

Library of Congress Cataloging in Publication Data

Main entry under title:
 Ethical perspectives on business and society.

 1. Political ethics—Addresses, essays, lectures. 2. Business ethics—Addresses, essays, lectures. 3. Social ethics—Addresses, essays, lectures. I. Kugel, Yerachmiel. II. Gruenberg, Gladys W.
JK1759.E8   170   77-3106
ISBN 0-669-01482-6

Copyright © 1977 by D.C. Heath and Company.

All rights reserved. No part of this publication may be reproduced or transmitted in any form or by any means, electronic or mechanical, including photocopy, recording, or any information storage or retrieval system, without permission in writing from the publisher.

Published simultaneously in Canada.

Printed in the United States of America.

International Standard Book Number: 0-669-01482-6

Library of Congress Catalog Card Number: 77-3106

Contents

	List of Contributors	vii
	Preface	ix
Chapter 1	Introduction: Models of Ethical Behavior *Yerachmiel Kugel* and *Gladys W. Gruenberg*	1
Part I	*Government and Society*	7
Chapter 2	The Challenge of the Ethical Dilemma	11
	2-1 American Ethics and the President *Amitai Etzioni*	11
	2-2 Restoring Faith in Government *Gerald R. Ford*	18
	2-3 Code of Ethics *Jimmy Carter*	20
Chapter 3	Some Specific Applications: Case Studies	23
	3-1 Statement on S. 1210, Federal Employees Disclosure Act of 1975 *William Proxmire*	23
	3-2 Statement Establishing Task Force on Questionable Corporate Payments Abroad *Gerald R. Ford*	27
	3-3 Position Paper on Ethical Perspectives *Elliot L. Richardson*	28
	3-4 Multinational Corporations and East Asia: The Foreign Policy Implications of the Lockheed Affair *Frank Church*	31
	3-5 Ethical Perspectives on Business and Society *Roderick M. Hills*	37
Part II	*Business and Society*	41
Chapter 4	The Ethical Debate	45
	4-1 Is Ethics Good Business? *Yerachmiel Kugel* and *Gladys W. Gruenberg*	45
	4-2 Business Faces Critics' Challenge *Irving Kristol*	50

Chapter 5	**Business' Response**	55
	5-1 Ethics—The Many Shades of Gray *William H. Wendel*	55
	5-2 Business Leadership and Moral Character *W. Michael Blumenthal*	61
	5-3 Public Trust in Business *Frank T. Cary*	65
	5-4 Corporate Reform: What's the Real Issue? *Irving S. Shapiro*	67
Chapter 6	**The Present Economic System and the Moral Dilemma**	77
	6-1 Ethical Confusion and the Business Community *Albert W. Levi*	77
	6-2 Towards New Corporate Goals: Co-existence with Society *Donald E. Schwartz*	84
	6-3 Sinful Structures: Society and Education *Robert J. Henle, S.J.*	104
Part III	*The Individual and Society*	115
Chapter 7	**Ethics and the Professions**	119
	7-1 Remarks Concerning the Science Court *Margaret Mead*	119
	7-2 The Role of the Lawyer in America *Sam J. Ervin, Jr.*	127
Chapter 8	**Conclusion: Ethical Guidelines for Decision Making** *Yerachmiel Kugel* and *Gladys W. Gruenberg*	133
	About the Editors	137

List of Contributors

W. Michael Blumenthal
Secretary of the Treasury
Former Chairman, Bendix Corporation

Jimmy Carter
President of the United States

Frank T. Cary
Chairman, International Business Machines Corporation

Frank Church
United States Senator

Sam J. Ervin, Jr.
Former United States Senator

Amitai Etzioni
Director, Center for Policy Research, Inc.
Professor of Sociology, Columbia University

Gerald R. Ford
Former President of the United States

Robert J. Henle, S.J.
McDonnell Professor of Justice in American Society, Saint Louis University
Former President, Georgetown University

Roderick M. Hills
Former Chairman, Securities and Exchange Commission
Chairman, Peabody Coal Company

Irving Kristol
Henry R. Luce Professor of Urban Values, New York University

Albert W. Levi
David May Distinguished University Professor of the Humanities, Washington University (Saint Louis)

Margaret Mead
Curator Emeritus, The American Museum of Natural History

William Proxmire
United States Senator

Elliot L. Richardson
Former Secretary of Commerce
Chairman, President's Task Force on Questionable Corporate Payments Abroad
Ambassador-at-Large, and Special Representative of the President for the Law of
    the Sea Conference

Irving S. Shapiro
Chairman, E.I. du Pont de Nemours and Company

Donald E. Schwartz
Professor of Law, Georgetown University

William H. Wendel
President, The Carborundum Company

Preface

In any discussion of ethical behavior, it is difficult to refrain from moralizing. However, it is becoming increasingly clear from the polls, news media, and other writings on the subject of professional conduct in the United States today, that a consensus is forming about the goals we seek as a civilized society and the means we are choosing to accomplish those goals. Particularly in public life, moral leadership is listed as the chief attribute that should characterize legislators and administrators, and more and more businessmen are speaking out to censure their colleagues for unethical business behavior.

Analysis of where we are and where we are headed is more profitable than recriminations about who is responsible for our ethical plight. While history can teach lessons about cause-and-effect relationships, too much concentration on living in the past and trying to bring back the good old days can blind us to the fact that there have been permanent changes in our social and economic environment which clearly prevent our return. Historically, men like Adam Smith and Thomas Jefferson believed in the ultimate perfectability of society through the perfectability of the individual.

When we began investigating the international payoff phenomenon, it became clear that the cost-benefit approach to individual ethical conduct is the most effective solution. Although it is individuals who are moral or immoral, institutions do influence individual ethical conduct by providing an array of incentives and disincentives for ethical behavior. Our contributors, who are representatives of academia, government, and business outline their thinking on the kinds of influences which are or should be imposed on individuals to insure better harmony between individual ethical conduct and societal goals.

If this book has any value, it is its universal appeal to the practitioner and student alike, arising from the smorgasbord approach we have taken to the subject of ethical conduct. This again squares with our belief, expressed in more detail in our book, *International Payoffs: Dilemma for Business*, that the individual executive is the bottom-line of all business decision making. The executive's conscience determines business morality or immorality. It has been our purpose to lay bare the myriad facets of the ethical decision-making process so that society may understand the depth of the problem and the breadth of insight that comes from seeking the solution.

Our special thanks go to all the participants in this cooperative venture. The caliber of the contributions is evidence of the high-level thought which is being brought to ethical questions. Basic moral values have returned to fashion; witness the passage of codes of ethical conduct in both the House and the Senate as the first order of business of the 1977 Congress, and the emphasis placed on the subject by the Carter administration. We are proud to be a part of the new order.

Again, we thank our families for their patience and tolerance during a trying period when we were immersed in the demands of manuscript deadlines and revisions. Our students also helped to bring immediate response to some of our thought processes. Part of the financial help came from the Beaumont Fund, and much of the moral support came from our faculty colleagues. To list all the influences which led to this finished product would read like an International Who's Who. We thank them, every one.

Saint Louis, Missouri

1977

Yerachmiel Kugel

Gladys W. Gruenberg

1 Introduction: Models of Ethical Behavior

Yerachmiel Kugel and
Gladys W. Gruenberg

As Theodore V. Purcell, S.J., states in his discussion of ethical business conduct, the first general principle is "do good and avoid evil."[1] It is in the application of that principle to specific actions that difficulty arises. There is a range of activities from "white" to "black" that is encountered every hour of every day. The white and the black activities are fairly easy to distinguish, and those who would act ethically can choose one and avoid the other. However, most human activity (and certainly most business decision making) falls somewhere between these extremes, in the area which we have called gray[2] in our discussion of international payoffs. William H. Wendel also applies this term to his analysis of business conduct.[3] It is in this gray area that decision making becomes a dilemma, particularly for the business executive who is torn between what he perceives as a profitable activity and what his conscience tells him is in the questionable, gray area of ethics. For the businessman this type of decision is an everyday occurrence, and the solution is ultimately determined by his own moral code.

In the interest of professional practice, the business executive considers all the possible consequences of his decisions, and acts in accordance with his long-run interest, and the long-run interest of the corporation which employs him. Similarly, the individual in public office considers his action in the light of the public interest as well as his own self-interest.

The public and private weal are tied together in society by the rule of law, so that unethical conduct is prohibited through legislation and violators are punished. Although some business leaders eschew conduct that is merely legal,[4] in our free society it is legal action which is permitted and illegal action which is frowned upon. This is especially important in a free market economy, since business firms in a competitive market need help from public policy to maintain standards of ethical behavior. (A word of caution is in order here. Competition as used in this book is not the competitive model of economic theory. It is more akin to the "workable" competition most businessmen talk about, that is quite imperfect according to economic model standards.)

In such a market system, regulation is necessary to establish certain minimum standards, so that legal (ethical?) conduct becomes equated with a firm's self-interest. Rather than interpreting legislation as censure, most firms welcome minimum regulation to make the burden (cost) of ethical decision making more equitable.[5] Normally, it is only the very large, very profitable firm that can afford to be ethical in the philanthropic sense. Operating in a monopoly market can also lessen the burden of ethical conduct. However, there is always the danger that regulation will become counterproductive and cause firms to evade legal obligations on the ground that harassment and red tape unnecessarily interfere with business activity. Some middle ground is desirable.

Some of our contributors suggest that a professional code of conduct should be adopted for business executives. Lack of uniform entrance requirements, and diversity of training and culture are often cited as drawbacks of such codes. The very pluralism which makes the United States a diversified market militates against uniform standards in the business community. However, through legislation on a limited basis, designed to accomplish minimum goals, business executives can be guided to fulfill society's aims without jeopardizing their own. In fact, it is our belief that the free market system can survive only in a civilized atmosphere of law and order. Jungle action by even a minority endangers the species. Marginal firms who manage to survive by "unfair" and illegal tactics are not essential to the free enterprise system any more than criminals are necessary to society. It is at the individual executive's level, however, where the final burden rests. Decisions which are compatible with both economics and ethics are not only possible but profitable if the proper incentives and disincentives are established by society.[6]

The contributions to this book have been divided into three categories determined by the major influences on individual ethical behavior: (1) government (legal), (2) business (economic), and (3) individual (moral values). Table 1-1 suggests the wide range of conduct possible for various professions, given the influences prescribed by each category. The business executive fits into any mold that he desires, and the cost-benefit approach helps him to make his decision.

This "map" of ethical options allows persons to determine where they stand and what model they want to choose as their own ethical goal. Whatever that decision is, they will find among the contributions here food for thought and guidance so that in the end they will be able to use the decision-making guidelines to their own advantage and that of their firm.

Notes

1. Theodore V. Purcell, S.J., "A Practical Guide to Ethics in Business," *Business and Society Review* (Spring 1975), pp. 46-50; reprinted in Yerachmiel Kugel and Gladys W. Gruenberg, *Selected Readings on International Payoffs* (Lexington, Mass.: D.C. Heath, 1977).

2. Yerachmiel Kugel and Gladys W. Gruenberg, *International Payoffs: Dilemma for Business* (Lexington, Mass.: D.C. Heath, 1977), Chapter 2.

3. William H. Wendel, "Ethics—The Many Shades of Gray," speech before

the Chemical Buyers Group, Purchasing Management Association, October 16, 1975; reprinted in chapter 5 of this book.

4. Cf. Caterpiller Tractor Co., *A Code of Worldwide Business Conduct*, October 1, 1974, p. 8; reprinted in Kugel and Gruenberg, *Selected Readings on International Payoffs*.

5. Cf. Bob Dorsey's (Gulf Oil Corporation) testimony before the Senate Subcommittee on Multinational Corporations, *Hearings*, Part 12, May-September 1975, p. 13.

6. Cf. Kugel and Gruenberg, *International Payoffs: Dilemma for Business*, Chapter 7.

Table 1-1
Models of Ethical Behavior

Model Number	1	2	3	4
Classification	Illegal and/or Unethical		Legal and/or Ethical	
General	Totally self-interest oriented.	Mainly self-oriented but legal.	Self-interest, P-R morality.	Self-sacrifice; total dedication to common good.
Specific:				
A. Moral	No moral consideration.	No moral consideration unless penalty.	Moral only for P-R purposes.	Morality in toto.
B. Legal	No legal consideration.	Will avoid obeying law unless severe penalty.	Obeys letter of law.	Obeys spirit of law. Initiates legal reform.
C. Economic	Money the only good—an end in itself.	Money most important goal.	Money important—some social considerations for P-R.	Social considerations paramount—money only means to end.
	Only short-run consideration (immediate gratification).	Mostly short-run considerations.	Some long-run considerations for P-R purposes.	Only long-run considerations (self-gratification postponed).
	Profession viewed only as monetary reward.	Minimum professionalism. Rewards paramount.	Professionalism for P-R purposes.	Total professionalism. Sense of mission.
Stereotyped Professions	Prostitutes, Drug pushers	Sexual surrogates, Gamblers	Businessmen, Politicians	Priests, Artists
Specific Professions		*Specific Models of Professionalism*		
Professor	Obtained degree by fraud. Dispenses false knowledge. Falsifies research.	Student involvement only when imposed. Lectures merely business. Quantity of research more important than quality.	Student involvement as P-R tool. Research only for personal reward.	Total student involvement. Sense of truth mission. Pure research.

Physician	Performs illegal operations for fee.	Limits practice to wealthy patients. Accepts kickbacks from suppliers.	Accepts poor patients for image purposes. Rejects kickbacks but condones practice.	Healing mission above reward. Rejects even referral fees.
Attorney	Mouthpiece for underworld. Client protection for fee.	Keeps silent. Uses confidentiality as screen. Law avoidance.	Resigns for P-R purposes. Emphasis on letter of law.	Initiates public disclosure. Implements spirit of law.
Journalist	On the take—paid to dispense false information.	Yellow journalism. Publication criterion—what will sell. Accepts all advertising.	Pays lip service to public service. May refuse some crass advertising for P-R purposes.	Sense of mission as public conscience. Truth determines coverage. Refuses advertising in poor taste.
Politician	Spy activities against public interest for foreign power.	Promotes legislation for personal interest.	Looks upon gratuities as good P-R.	Disowns all personal interest. Devotes self to public service.
Business Executive	Engages in secret bribes in violation of law.	Payoffs at all levels of activity if no severe penalty. No code of ethics.	Pays small sums to get things done but image important. Code of ethics for P-R purposes.	No gratuities of any kind. Code of ethics strictly enforced. Disclosure of all activities in public interest.
Accountant	Facilitates bribery.	Remains silent, uses confidentiality as screen.	Resigns for P-R purposes.	Public disclosure in public interest.
Director	Hides information on bribery. Gives false information under investigation.	Believes that business is business, incompatible with social norms.	Meets social norms under pressure.	Anticipates social norms.

Source: Reprinted from Yerachmiel Kugel and Gladys W. Gruenberg, *International Payoffs: Dilemma for Business* (Lexington, Mass.: Lexington Books, D.C. Heath and Company, 1977), chapter 6.

Note: The authors acknowledge ideas obtained from Max Lerner, et al., *Saturday Review*, November 1975, and S. Prakash Sethi, *California Management Review*, Spring 1975, which were used in developing this table.

Part I
Government and Society

Introduction to Part I

Government determines the ground rules for business conduct both by moral leadership and positive legislation. Individual business executives take their cue from the moral tone set by the national administration. As Watergate so aptly proved, corruption at the top sifts down throughout the moral fiber of the community. Amitai Etzioni expands on this theme by describing the moral crisis in the United States and the President's role in leading citizens to achieve moral and spiritual objectives.

President Gerald Ford understood this challenge when he took office and undertook on many occasions to stress his desire to "restore public confidence in government." A more detailed program to restore public confidence in government is seen in President Jimmy Carter's code of ethics.

Senator William Proxmire deals with a specific aspect of restoring public confidence in government by insisting that government must institutionalize whistle-blowing to increase morality, since individuals who act in accordance with their consciences need protection from retaliation (disincentive) for such behavior. Whistle-blowing increases the possibility of detection, thereby increasing the cost of immorality.

Adding to his general determination to bring integrity to government, President Ford was specifically interested in investigating one of the foremost harbingers of business immorality, international payoffs or "questionable payments" as he preferred to call them. In setting up his Task Force on Questionable Corporate Payments Abroad, President Ford called for disclosure as a first step toward public censure of unethical behavior in the business community.

SEC Chairman Roderick Hills reinforced this attitude by his leadership in encouraging voluntary disclosure of such payments through the normal process of business reporting required under the Securities Exchange Act of 1934. Hills' contribution explains his philosophy in connection with this decision.

Senator Frank Church discusses the Lockheed affair, and points out how multinational corporations interfere with United States foreign policy and jeopardize international relations by threatening the party in power with justifiable allegations of conflict of interest. This is another reason for government intervention.

Secretary of Commerce Elliot Richardson, Chairman of the President's Task Force on Questionable Corporate Payments Abroad, gives his reasons for the moral lapse in the international market and offers legislative proposals for its correction.

These practical cases involving varying aspects of business moral behavior give an insight into the specific areas of business conduct which need control to minimize the adverse impact on society's moral climate, economic viability, and relations with other societies.

2 The Challenge of the Ethical Dilemma

2-1 American Ethics and the President

Amitai Etzioni

An unusual and possibly unique feature of this year's presidential election campaign is the emergence of the condition of American ethics as one of the pivotal issues, vying for voter attention with such classic concerns as peace and prosperity. Though a recent national poll recorded that only 19% of Americans cited morality as a major source of concern (as opposed to 53% who listed inflation and 34% unemployment), two of every three Americans (67%) felt that "people do not lead as good lives—honest and moral—as they used to." Since this view was held by only 52% of those polled in 1965 and 46% in 1952, the public seems to sense a serious erosion of morality.

The rather bitter flavor Americans are feeling on the subject is illustrated by another recent survey which found 85% of a national sample agreeing either "partly" or "strongly" that "people who work hard don't get a fair break." And practically every day brings a new report of unethical conduct by a Congressman, a corporation, physicians, accountants, lawyers, and in most other occupations and walks of life.

What is the nature of the ethical problem? Can we agree about what is ethical? Is there a crisis or just greater attention to incidents of unethical conduct? What role, if any, can and should the President of the United States play in dealing with ethical issues?

What is Ethical?

Can ethics be defined? Is it not a personal, subcultural, or religious matter—what one person or group deems a moral issue, others do not? When this matter was explored at a recent meeting of the American Press Institute, I was taken aback when an editor asked me about the "morality" of printing four-letter words in his small town newspaper. I could barely see a moral (or ethical) issue in this. On the one hand, a Republican elder statewoman expresses the sentiments of conservative members of the community when she refers in a single breath to increased sexual permissiveness, crime, defiance of authority, and "religiouslessness" all as signs of moral decay. On the other hand, left-liberals tend to stress the immorality of the establishment, abuse of power, and the injustices of poverty, racism, and sexism.

For the social scientist, at least for this one, the most important point is that all these varying concepts of morality hide one principle, that, despite their differences, all share acceptance of a set of rules, an ethical code. The main function of such a code, whatever its specific context, is to civilize life; to make members of society treat others the way they wish others would treat them—as persons, not as objects or instruments. While this ideal is never fully attained, it is advanced by the formulations of rules of conduct which define do's and don't's, which tell people what is considered "fair" or "right" and what is not. On the taboo side are basically acts of excessive self-interest and abuse of others (as individuals or as communities). The do's tend to concern doing one's share in helping others and in carrying out communal duties. By this criterion four-letter words and premarital sex, for instance, are unethical only if they truly offend those involved—that is, if disrespect, embarrassment, or humiliation is the result. Otherwise, they are matters of manner and personal choice. In contrast, economic exploitation and most crimes are immoral by definition because they entail abuse of others for the advantage of the perpetrator.

Radicals correctly point out that a society's rules reflect its power structure. Thus, typically, Americans are more concerned about offenses against private property than are members of, say, a kibbutz. However, all this tells us is that a particular set of rules may well be questioned or changed; it does not follow that a society without any rules can be civil, or indeed can survive.

The Scope of the Moral Crisis

The polls cited above leave no doubt that most Americans perceive a moral decline. This is significant because, even if the decline were only "in the eyes of the beholder" (unlike a scarcity of resources or even the fear of crime), belief is a major factor. If most people feel that those around them do not play by the rules and get away with it, this is one main reason many of them will act unethically. On the other hand, a sense that most people do behave is one of the reasons many forms of unethical conduct become unthinkable for most members of such fortunate communities. For example, stealing is believed to have been very rare in traditional Eskimo tribes, though there were neither cops nor jails; it was just too terrible an act for most Eskimos to even consider.

Precise data on the actual level of unethical conduct in the U.S. are hard to come by. Understandably, their own wrong-doing is a subject people are disinclined to report and record. Actually it matters little whether the exact proportion of those who violate the rules in this or that area of conduct is 40%, 50%, or 60%. The main sociological issue is whether unethical conduct is exceptional, characteristic of a submajority, or prevalent.

Exceptional unethical conduct is found in all communities, including monasteries, Puritan towns, and religious zealot settlements. The shock and dismay generated by misconduct in these places are a sign that the community's ethical antibodies are in fine condition. When unethical conduct is prevalent, like bribery in many developing nations, it is only barely viewed as immoral, and this tolerance becomes one main reason such behavior is especially difficult to counter. Similarly, many nations in which police brutality, domestic spying, and other abuses of government power are common find it inexplicable that people in the U.S. could become so wrought up over Watergate. Once the rules are disregarded to the point that their existence is widely questioned, it is difficult to revitalize them short of radical surgery.

Unethical behavior among a significant submajority occurs in-between, when respect for rules has weakened but not crumbled, when more and more people act in ways previously considered almost unthinkable; but they and the others are still reflective of their behavior and are, to varying degrees, guilty about their misconduct. Because the rules still retain some binding force, a return to a community (within which breaches are exceptional) is still possible. However, as in other processes of erosion, once minor trickles turn into substantial streams, fingers in the dike are no longer sufficient. Either major shoring-up must be effected, or the tiny leaks will rapidly turn into a major torrent. To put it differently, unethicality among the submajority is what the sociologists call an "unsteady state"; either the ethical code will regain wide support or further, more extensive breakdowns in observance of the rules will ensue. It is not possible to maintain for long a situation in which the populus is expected to respect and abide by the laws when large numbers of people get away with clear and frequent violations of the code.

The U.S., at present, seems precisely in this middle, transitional category of unethicality among the submajority in many areas of conduct. One comes to this conclusion indirectly, via the stream of incidents reported in the press daily, and more directly from the incidence of unethical behaviors for which some statistical data are available. Thus, while not all violations of the law are necessarily unethical, most crimes are.

The number of persons in the U.S. who have engaged in crime runs into the millions, and studies show that millions of others have been or are involved in similar crimes for which they are not caught. The list of major U.S. corporations engaged in acts of bribery, many of which have a domestic dimension (such as illegal deduction of expenses from taxes and misstatements during audits) shows that such behavior is certainly no longer exceptional but involves a significant submajority of *Fortune*'s list of 500 major U.S. corporations.

The number of physicians engaged in unnecessary surgery ranges somewhere between 15% and 30%—certainly more than an exceptional practice. Nursing home owners may be the first group to openly go over the top, with more than half of them charged with serious abuses. And so it goes, from payola (still quite common in the liquor and record industries) to auto repairs, grain inspection, police corruption, purchase of term papers on campuses, and so on.

As far as institutions are concerned, some serious violations have been reported involving the Presidency, Congress, and government agencies such as the FBI, CIA and IRS; labor unions (recently, the Teamsters), and political parties (e.g., the charges of bribery and corruption leveled against the chairman of the Democratic Party in New York State). Those relatively spared so far, e.g., the churches and universities, may perhaps be made of sterner stuff—or their defrocking is merely yet to come.

In the vast majority of unethical instances, individual or institutional, exposed so far the unethical conduct goes well beyond anything that could be called trivial or marginal (such as not returning the excess change to the clerk at the grocery store; failing to report the money made from a garage sale in one's income tax return; or whatever is the corporate, government, and union equivalent of such offenses). Rather, unethical conduct was found to pervade the central pursuits of the person or organization: surgery for surgeons, election and separation of power for the Presidency, and so on.

Since the uncovering of the Watergate cover-ups, the nation has been led from the exposure of one tawdry event to a confrontation with another, to an anxious awareness of a deep and pervasive societal crisis. The momentum of this more general crisis lies in a slow decomposition of the ethical fabric and seems due to many causes, including an acceleration of societal change since World War II; an increase in conflict about what is right and wrong due to the increased integration of social groups of divergent subcultures and values into the mainstream of America; and a gradual disintegration of respect for authority, whether parental, public, or institutional.

While it cannot be proved beyond reasonable doubt that unethical conduct is on the rise and has reached substantial though not prevalent dimensions, it seems on the basis of available evidence to be more than exceptional, more than a matter of isolated incidents. As far as this sociologist can observe, we may be nearing a tipping point. Unless we undertake a more active and effective role in the shoring-up of our ethical foundations, the rising cynicism may break down the ethical code, leaving the civic order to be a matter largely of policing. This would be extremely detrimental, as the police mechanisms (not just cops, but also inspectors, auditors, etc.) suffice only when most people most of the time do what is right without being policed because they accept the code. When the system tries to rely on policing, it tends to break down in the sense that the costs of policing compete severely with the resources needed for other social purposes and no effective civic order can be maintained.

What Is To Be Done?

It might be argued, quite justifiably, that "what is to be done?" is the wrong question. Ethics cannot be designed, manufactured, ordered by the yard, imported, and distributed. Ethical codes gradually emerge, or fail to emerge, out of billions of personal decisions, dialogues, experiences. And yet, when the social-historical conditions are ripe for moral leadership to assert itself, a nation's mood and orientation can be changed to provide a more positive setting for these myriad personal decisions.

The U.S. may be ripe for such an ethical restoration. People seem increasingly weary of public scandals; they yearn for positive identification and commitment—of an authentic, not demagogic sort—and they seek to return to an era of more stable values, of a clearer and more positive national and personal self-image. The most successful candidates in recent elections have been those who have both impressed the public with their own personal integrity and trustworthiness, and who have put forward as the central task to be accomplished the recreation of an America—and an American way of life—that Americans can believe in and be proud of in a spiritual and not just material sense.

What Can the President Do?

It has recently become fashionable to favor a less active—and indeed a weaker—presidency, as well as one less surrounded by regal rituals. This view is often advanced in terms of doing away with the imperial president. It is usually coupled with a preference for greater decision making on the part of Congress or by the people themselves. While both developments are desirable, it does not follow that the president can or should be without a role of moral leadership. For better or worse, the way the American government is set up, the president has and will continue to have a tremendous model-setting and agenda-forming power.

As long as there is one president who is simultaneously the head of state, chief of staff, and in charge of the executive branch, while there are 535 members of Congress divided against each other and administering little more than their own staffs; the presidency will be the focus of public attention, of the media, of the political give and take, and of the other institutions, including Congress itself. Even if we did away with regal airs, all White House dinners were henceforth cancelled, the Marine band ceased to play "Hail to the Chief," and the Rose Garden were plowed over, the president of the United States would continue to hold the post of the nation's head. And many Americans would continue to identify with the president as *the* national leader, and he would continue to have a great capacity to influence the nation by the personal example he sets and by the issues he chooses to emphasize . . . or ignore.

As a person upon whom the nation's attention is focused, the president is widely emulated. When it was reported shortly before tax-filing time in 1974 that President Nixon had vastly reduced his payments by predating a gift certificate of his papers donated to the National Archives, IRS agents all over the nation reported that nearly every citizen they saw stated, implied, or suggested that, if the president of the United States could cheat on his taxes.... Studies of school children show that in the Eisenhower and Kennedy years the presidency was highly idealized and the president viewed as unable to do any wrong; identification with him led children to aspire to act nobly themselves. In recent years, children tend to view the president as putting himself above the law, corrupt, and otherwise unworthy. They also see less reason why they should act ethically.

Thus, the emulation factor cuts both ways. If the president sets a higher example, this could be one factor in reversing ethical cynicism. This can be achieved most directly in personal matters that are common to all citizens (President Ford's and several presidential candidates' release of their tax returns is a good example; firing cabinet and staff members only for cause and not for political expediency is another.)

Second, the abuse of power—a main form of presidential violation of the rules—must be clearly, demonstrably stopped. Thus, if the president were really to end abuse of the FBI, CIA, IRS, the Post Office, and other governmental agencies used in the past for purposes of harassment and worse; and if this action were made both visible and believable through reports of effective watchdog commissions (including not just Congressmen but also eminent citizens whom the public trusts, such as Ralph Nader and John Gardner), public confidence in the integrity of the government could gradually be restored. Corporate executives, accountants, lawyers, and physicians would then be more inclined to clean up their professional and personal houses; at the least they could no longer avail themselves of presidential lawlessness as an easy excuse.

The president also has considerable power to set the agenda for the nation—to define the issues we focus upon and the ways we approach them. Truman's ushering in of the Cold War era, and Kennedy's and Johnson's concern with civil rights, come under the rubric of presidential agenda-setting. The president-elect could put the shoring-up of America's ethics in a high place on the nation's agenda by including in his inaugural address and first State of the Union message not only proposals on economic, social, and foreign-policy matters but the suggestion of steps for curbing unethical behavior, and encouraging ethical conduct, both in government and in the society at large. Which specific measures should be advanced is a subject for lengthy consideration, but the basic approach can be illustrated quickly.

Role of the Government

First, laws which are not enforced should either be enforced or removed from the books. Unenforced laws are a social poison not just because the matter they seek to regulate is left unregulated, but because they undermine the credibility of the civic order, which spills over into those matters not directly expressed in law, the ethical code. It is senseless, for instance, to make millions of Americans who consume marijuana into law-breakers, or to allow people to use marijuana but penalize those who sell it. Even traffic laws (e.g., 55 mph speed limit) should either be more systematically enforced or modified (e.g., raise the speed limit). Otherwise, the wide violation of the law serves as a kind of school for unethical conduct, and the lessons so learned do in turn gradually transfer from one area of conduct to others.

Second, penalties exacted for the same violation in different parts of the country or by different judges must be equalized, or at least be less unequal. People tend to behave when they feel the system of sanctions is fundamentally fair; they tend to rebel when they sense it to be arbitrary. Study after study has shown that different judges in the same court, and different courts across the nation, mete out radically different sentences to persons who have committed the same offense. Less leeway to judges through legislation requiring standardized sentences may help restore a sense of fair play.

Third, the intrusion of special interest, which bends public life to a privileged few, must be curbed. Various bills to limit the opportunities for illegitimate political influence have been suggested on the state and federal levels, but few have been enacted and even fewer are enforced.

Next, the president might challenge Congress to a higher level of ethical conduct. If Congress were put sufficiently in the limelight, it might act more vigorously against members who abuse their offices. The context could be set by requiring disclosure of all private interests and sources of income, and by prohibiting any income from outside sources. Next to the president, members of Congress are the most important source of leadership on issues involving civic morality. If they were to set a better example, state legislators and city council members might follow suit, along with "front-line" public servants such as policemen, building inspectors, Medicaid auditors, followed by the professions, the corporations, and the public at large.

Corporations could be required to disclose more of their activities, to adhere to a new, more explicitly stated code of ethics and, as a senator has suggested, to open their records to outside audit committees, or include on their boards of directors one or more publicly appointed members. Also, as Ralph Nader has suggested, the lax local corporation charters might be replaced by more stringent federal ones.

Conference of Educators

Nor need the president limit his leadership to acting as a role model, agenda-setting, and putting forward draft legislation. A White House conference of educators should be convened to work on ways moral education in schools can be furthered. The schools are pivotal for several reasons: first, because to the extent to which we are witnessing widespread break-up of the U.S. family or its defection from the duty of developing the moral character of children, the schools, as the main alternate source of guidance, gain in importance in this capacity. Also, they are more subject to influence via public policy and more accountable to the community than are the myriad families. However, many schools, by encouraging winning (rather than playing fair) in sports, by condoning cheating in exams and homework, by disregarding many acts of extortion and vandalism, are the place millions in the U.S. experience and internalize the idea that playing by the rules is *not* the way to make it. Unless these formative experiences are reversed, there is little hope for a renaissance of adult civic ethicality.

These steps, and others like them, will in and of themselves not build an ethical community, but they may serve to set a new tone, a new mood, in which individuals, parents, educators, citizens, will be more willing and more able to do their restorative work. Recently, President Ford suggested that the time has arrived to put Watergate behind us, to stop torturing ourselves with ever more revelations of abuses and scandals. Such a healing is needed; but, if it is attempted before significant reforms are carried out in the work of the public institutions and public attitudes, the result will be to suppress from consciousness the spread of unethical conduct and allow it, again, to grow out of sight, until one day in the not too remote future, unethical conduct will seem prevalent, a condition far from unknown in earlier historical periods or on other continents, but one we have long sought to avoid in this nation.

2-2 Restoring Faith in Government

Gerald R. Ford

**Remarks at Montgomery County
Historical Society Museum, June 7, 1976**

First, we have restored confidence and trust in the White House. This administration has been open, it has been candid, it has been forthright, and as a result the American people, instead of being divided, are united. They have faith in the Oval Office, they have faith in the president.

**Remarks at GOP Reception,
Springfield, Missouri, June 11, 1977**

I would like to take a very few minutes to talk positively and affirmatively about the record of the Ford Administration for the last 22 months. Refresh your memory just a bit. In August of 1974 this country was in serious trouble for reasons that we all know. There had been a great loss of confidence in the White House itself. This country was facing economic chaos in August of 1974. We were suffering 12 percent or higher inflation. We were on the brink of the worst economic recession in 40 years. We were still in war. Our allies were uncertain and our adversaries were tempted. In the last 22 months we have turned all three around.

We have restored confidence and trust in the White House by the fact that we have had an open, straightforward, candid administration. The door is open to individuals, the door is open to people who will come in and work with us, bring us their criticism, their complaints and their recommendations.

The net result is the White House is trusted. The White House has had a restoration of confidence.

**President's News Conference,
July 19, 1976**

*Legislative Proposal to Restore Confidence in
the Government*

Q. Mr. President, that Watergate reform bill, the Senate version of it goes to the floor today. Until last week the administration, I gather, was very much opposed to it. Now you are in with a major proposal to change it. Can you tell us how the administration came up with these proposals at the 11th hour?

The President. The administration has had many reservations about several of the provisions in the bill that is on the floor of the Senate at the present time. One, the Senate bill provides, as we understand it—and we have gone into it with some outstanding legal scholars—an unconstitutional method of the appointment of a special prosecutor.

So, what we have recommended is a completely constitutional method of selecting a special prosecutor, one that would call for a special prosecutor recommended by the president, confirmed by the Senate for a 3-year term, with that particular special prosecutor being ineligible to serve other than the first 3 years.

That is definitely a constitutional way to have a Special Prosecutor who would have criminal authority over any allegations made against a president, a vice president, high executive officials, all members of Congress, and those involved in the judiciary.

Our reservation was not as to the thrust but as to the constitutionality of several provisions, including the one I have just described.

Q. What is your proposal?

The President. Well, it is our proposal that we feel would accomplish the job of restoring public confidence in all three branches of the federal government and do it in a constitutional way.

2-3 Code of Ethics

Jimmy Carter

The two questions I hear again and again across this country are: "Can our government be competent?" "Can our government be honest and decent and open?" I have to say that a majority of people would say, "no." This is the first since polling was started that a majority of our people say that our national and economic status will be worse in 5 years than it is now. But we don't need to be pessimistic.

I have run the Georgia government in a tough, businesslike way. As a scientist, businessman, planner and farmer, I've managed it tightly and brought about some dramatic changes in its costs, long-range planning and budgeting techniques and organizational structure. We cut administrative costs more than 50% in Georgia. We abolished 278 out of 300 agencies and departments. So, I know it is possible to run an efficient government.

We ought not to lower our standards in government. Our government in Washington ought to be an inspiration to us all and not a source of shame. I want to spell out to you a number of things that can be done:

An all-inclusive "Sunshine Law" similar to those passed in several states, should be implemented in Washington. Meetings of federal boards, commissions and regulatory agencies must be opened to the public, along with those of congressional committees. The only exceptions should involve narrowly defined national security issues, unproven legal accusations or knowledge that might cause serious damage to the nation's economy.

Broad public access, consonant with the right of personal privacy, should be provided to government files. Maximum security declassification must be implemented.

The activities of lobbyists must be more thoroughly revealed and controlled, both within Congress and the executive department agencies. The new lobbying law should apply to those executive agencies and departments which are not now covered as well as to the Congress. Quarterly reports of expenditures by all lobbyists who spend more than $250 in lobbying in any three month period should be required. The act should include any lobbying expenditures aimed at influencing legislation or executive decisions and should cover those who lobby directly, solicit others to lobby or employ lobbyists in their own behalf.

The sweetheart arrangement between regulatory agencies and the regulated industries must be broken up, and the revolving door between them should be closed. Federal legislation should restrict the employment of any member of a regulatory agency by the industry being regulated.

All requests for special government consideration by private or corporate interests should be made public, and decisions should be made only on the basis of merit.

Complete revelation of all business and financial involvement of all major officials should be required, and none should be continued which constitute a possible conflict with the public interest. I have released an audit of my personal finances and will do so annually throughout my term of office. I will insist that the same requirement apply to the vice president and to those appointed to major policy-making positions in my administration. As president, I will seek legislation to make such disclosure mandatory.

Everyone who serves in a position of policy-making ought to reveal to the public his or her financial holdings, where his or her riches are invested and where his or her special interests are so that no conflict with the public interest will exist.

Public financing of campaigns should be extended to members of Congress.

Fines for illegal campaign contributions have often been minimal. They should be at least equal to the amount of the illegal donation.

Absolutely no gifts of value should ever again be permitted to a public official. A report of all minor personal gifts should be made public.

All diplomats, federal judges and other major officials should be selected on a strict basis of merit.

Independent, blue-ribbon, judicial selection commissions should be established to recommend persons considered best qualified for appointment as federal judges and prosecutors, and, as president, I will make my selection from those recommended.

The attorney general and all his or her assistants should be barred from any political activity. He or she should be given the full prerogatives and authority and independence that were recently given to the special prosecutor. The attorney general should be appointed by the president, with the confirmation of the Senate, and should not be removed except for malfeasance.

During the campaign, and as president, I will make myself available to the news media. Press conferences will be held monthly or more often throughout my administration.

I will propose to the Congress that the members of my Cabinet appear regularly before both Houses, preferably in joint session, to answer questions from Senators and Representatives. I will also request that these sessions be available for live broadcast.

Requests to the IRS for income tax returns by anyone, from the President down, should be recorded. Access to this essentially private information should be strictly circumscribed.

Maximum personal privacy for private citizens should be guaranteed.

As president, I will be responsible for the conduct of the executive branch of government. Errors of malfeasance will be immediately revealed, and an explanation given to the public, along with corrective action to prevent any recurrence of such actions. The same responsibility for campaign actions will be assumed by me as a candidate.

There is only one person in this nation who can speak with a clear voice, who can set a standard of morals and decency and openness, who can spell out comprehensive policies and coordinate the efforts of different departments of government, who can call on the American people for sacrifices and explain the purpose of that sacrifice and the consequences of it. *That person is the president.* The president ought to be personally responsible for everything that goes on in the executive branch of government, whether that be the appointment of major officials, the clear description of policy, the relationship of the executive with Congress, the revelation of mistakes and mismanagement, if any, or violations of the law, should they occur, unfairness on the part of regulatory agencies and so forth.

3 Some Specific Applications: Case Studies

3-1 Statement on S. 1210, Federal Employees Disclosure Act of 1975

William Proxmire

Mr. Chairman, I am very pleased to appear this morning to talk about ways to protect the rights of government employees in telling the public the truth about the public's business. I support S. 1210, the Federal Employees Disclosure Act of 1975, and I warmly congratulate you for introducing that bill and holding these hearings.

In addition to the relief provided government employees in S. 1210, I would like to propose the establishment of a special prosecutor's office to prosecute officials who violate the laws designed to protect employees who testify before congressional committees.

We have seen, in the series of abuses associated with Watergate, how reluctant the Justice Department can be when it comes to enforcing laws that are violated by persons in high places in the Executive Branch of the government.

The Justice Department has demonstrated the same reluctance with regard to federal employees whose rights have been consistently violated with respect to the disclosure of information before committees of Congress.

These violations of law have also seriously impaired the ability of members of Congress and committees to obtain information necessary to perform the functions set out in the Constitution.

In addition, Congress is not able to perform fully its constitutional role if it cannot obtain from federal employees the same kind of cooperation and candid opinions given by private citizens.

In view of the tremendous complexity and size of our federal government and the growing complexity, I think that it is most important to take steps to ensure that we get the kind of information that we must have if we are going to be able to prevent corruption and waste in government.

I feel very strongly that the best way to do that is to get from people who are involved in government, who are responsible for the course of the governmental action with the experts who work on it day after day. If they are prevented from speaking their minds and complaining and blowing the whistle, then I think the prospects of running an efficient and honest government are enormously reduced.

It is understandable that bureau chiefs and agency heads try to maintain a certain amount of control and supervision over the operations of their employees. This is desirable, up to a point. I am sure that there is no intent on your part, Mr. Chairman, nor is it mine to do anything to disrupt the orderly activities of the executive agencies.

But, the needs of government agencies must give way to the overriding need of the public and Congress to know the facts about the conduct of the public's business whenever the two come into conflict.

I have a considerable amount here in my experience with the Fitzgerald case and the C-5(A), and the ordeal that Mr. Fitzgerald has gone through in connection with the C-5(A). I might stress that all Mr. Fitzgerald did was commit truth at a hearing just like this one when he appeared before the subcommittee of the Joint Economic Committee, of which I was chairman, and he did not volunteer information about the C-5(A). He did not say that it had an overrun of $2 million. I asked him whether the overrun on C-5(A) could be as much as $2 million.

He had the choice of either lying, or telling the truth. He chose the truth. For that he has been hounded out of government. And, of course, he has conducted a historic fight of which you are undoubtedly aware.

I have gone into a little detail in my statement, which I will skip in the interest of time. Because of the lack of time, I will not go into detail on Mr. Fitzgerald's lengthy hearings before the Civil Service Commission, or the initial refusal of the commission to give Mr. Fitzgerald public hearings; his successful efforts in the courts of law that forced the commission to give a public hearing; his eventual vindication by the commission, which ruled he was wrongfully dismissed from the Air Force.

Mr. Fitzgerald was ordered reinstated with back pay but was not given his former job. He is now engaged in another action before the Civil Service Commission in appealing the Air Force's decision to assign him a lesser job with lesser responsibilities than those he formerly held.

Mr. Fitzgerald with the help of the American Civil Liberties Union which has provided him with free legal assistance, and through his own efforts managed to salvage all of his reputation and part of his career, but the expense was very great—very great to the lawyers who donated their services and to Mr. Fitzgerald, who had to bear thousands of dollars in expenses during the proceedings.

There are many other causes like Mr. Fitzgerald's. Most of the cases have ended far less satisfactorily because of the lack of resources available to fight this kind of injustice. Many have ended tragically with forced resignations, wrongful dismissals, and ruined careers.

Mr. Fitzgerald is one of the very, very few examples—and maybe the only example—in which a man has been able to fight back and maintain his career, in spite of the odds and the power against him.

Who has gained by the underhanded and unworthy attempts by officials in the Air Force to discredit an employee who told the truth about a cost overrun to a committee of Congress? Not the Air Force, not Mr. Fitzgerald, not Congress, and certainly not the public.

In addition, the problems imposed upon Mr. Fitzgerald, problems which are not completely resolved yet, have had a chilling effect on other employees of the government. This is, perhaps, what those officials in the Air Force responsible for the prosecution of Mr. Fitzgerald sought to achieve.

The lesson to other federal employees is clear: Do not disclose the facts about the expenditure of government funds, or about any other aspect of government programs, if they will embarrass your superiors or the head of your agency.

The guiding principle must be to keep the lid on all problems. Last year Mr. Fitzgerald again had to resort to the courts of law in order to obtain the rights being denied him by the Civil Service Commission in one of his appeals. The U.S. District Court for the District of Columbia ruled in his favor on July 15, 1974. The order issued by the court summarizes quite well the problems which this subcommittee is seeking to solve. Therefore, I will quote from the District Court's order:

"This case," said the District Court, "presents an exceptional history of unseemly delays and conduct by various agencies of the government. This conduct smacks of harrassment and vindictiveness towards an individual who dared to expose the shortcomings of his superiors. Whether deliberately or not, it will intimidate others who might feel duty-bound to take similar actions. It is now four and one-half years since the plaintiff has had initial separation."

Mr. Chairman, this is no way to run a republic. The actions against this individual have been undemocratic, underhanded, and unproductive. The question is, what steps should be taken by Congress to prevent such miscarriages of justice and denials of the rights of individuals and the Congress and the public from recurring?

As I stated earlier, I support the pending bill, which would recognize the rights of federal employees to disclose any information obtainable under the Freedom of Information Act, and which would give employees the right to seek justice in the courts of law for acts of intimidation taken against them by the government, rather than going through a lengthy and sometimes torturous procedure in the Civil Service Commission.

Frankly, Mr. Chairman, I would go further in the bill. With your permission, I would like finally to suggest several ways to strengthen your bill.

The problem is not only that government employees suffer at the hands of their superiors and that these employees need to be protected. The problem is also that those who engage in reprisals must be deterred.

At present, employees who tell the truth are punished, while the officials who retaliate against them are rewarded. This upside-down system of reward and punishment is apparent in the Fitzgerald case, where the military aid who informed against him untruthfully was promoted to the rank of general, and the Air Force secretary who wrongfully fired him has since been given another presidential appointment.

Meanwhile, the victim has been only partially compensated and is still involved in Civil Service Commission proceedings. I therefore propose that the law protecting citizens who testify before Congressional committees be amended to provide:

1. that the Department of Justice be required to promptly investigate any complaint of a citizen alleging violation of Section 1505 of Title 14 of the U.S. Code; then the determination would be made within six months as to whether or not prosecution is warranted.

I might point out, Mr. Chairman, that after waiting for a year for the Department of Justice to act, I got up on the floor of the Senate every day—I should say every month, for several months—pointing out that another month had gone by without any action by the Department of Justice to enforce the law, although the law clearly had been violated against Mr. Fitzgerald.

If the Department of Justice decides not to prosecute, a report must be written as to why the decision was reached. This is what I am proposing. And, that a copy would be supplied to the citizen who complained and the individual in question.

In the event that the Department of Justice decides not to prosecute, the citizen or individual in question may petition the appropriate District Court for an order to compel prosecution. The District Court may then hold a hearing, and if it finds sufficient evidence to warrant a prosecution does exist, the court will refer the matter to the special prosecutor in order to take the case.

If we agree that the gagging of government employees through harrassment is a significant problem, we should agree that significant steps should be taken by Congress to solve this problem.

These steps should include measure to deal with both sides of the difficulty. On the one hand, government employees are made to suffer, and they must be given more effective remedies than now exist.

Your bill does that by giving employees access to the courts. On the other hand, this is what I would add. Some government officials—the higher-ups—are getting away with bureaucratic murder. There is no sanction to prevent them from persecuting those who want to be candid and truthful. We have seen how ineffective the Department of Justice is when it comes to investigating wrongdoing within the executive branch of the federal government.

For this reason I conclude that it is necessary to go outside the Justice Department—outside the executive branch—to provide an appropriate remedy to the problems that now exist.

3-2 Statement Establishing Task Force on Questionable Corporate Payments Abroad

Gerald R. Ford

Recent disclosures that American-based corporations have made questionable payments during the course of their overseas operations have raised substantial public policy issues here at home.

The federal government is already undertaking a number of firm actions to deal with this matter. Full-scale investigations to determine whether U.S. laws have been violated are currently underway in the Securities and Exchange Commission, the Internal Revenue Service, and elsewhere. In addition, I have directed my advisers in the areas of foreign policy and international trade to work with other governments abroad in seeking to develop a better set of guidelines for all corporations.

To ensure that our approach to this issue is both comprehensive and properly coordinated, I am today establishing a cabinet-level Task Force on Questionable Corporate Payments Abroad.

The task force will be chaired by the Secretary of Commerce, Elliot Richardson, and it will include among its members the Secretaries of State, Treasury and Defense as well as the Attorney General and other high-ranking members of the administration.

I have directed the task force to conduct a sweeping policy review of this matter and to recommend such additional policy steps as may be warranted. The views of the broadest base of interest groups and individuals are to be solicited as part of this effort. I have also asked that periodic progress reports be submitted to me during the course of the review, and that a final report be on my desk before the end of the current calendar year.

The purpose of this task force is not to punish American corporations, but to ensure that the U.S. has a clear policy and that we have an effective, active program to implement that policy.

To the extent that the questionable payments abroad have arisen from corrupt practices on the part of American corporations, the United States bears a clear responsibility to the entire international community to bring them to a halt. Corrupt business practices strike at the very heart of our own moral code and our faith in free enterprise. Businesses in this country run the risk of ever greater governmental regulation if they illegally take advantage of consumers, investors and taxpayers.

Before we condemn American citizens out of hand, however, it is essential that we also recognize the possibility that some of the questionable payments abroad may result from extortion by foreign interests. To the extent that such practices exist, I believe that the United States has an equal responsibility to our own businesses to protect them from strong-arm practices. It is incumbent upon us to work with foreign governments to curb any such abuses.

From the facts at hand it is not clear to me where true justice lies in this matter, and that issue may never be resolved to everyone's satisfaction. The central policy question that needs to be addressed today is rather how we can arrive at clear, enforceable standards to prevent such questionable activities in the future. That is the key issue to which this new task force will direct its attentions.

3-3 Position Paper on Ethical Perspectives

Elliot L. Richardson

In America today, instead of the clearly defined and deeply rooted moral precepts that supported the Republic's founding and growth, we have a shifting moral impressionism that fails to perform the fundamental function of morality—the strengthening of the bonds of community and the assurance of communitarian continuity. Instead of public standards of ethical behavior, we have flexible personal positions. Instead of principles, we have private rationalizations.

We can see this drift in the declining respect for institutions and institutional authority, and we can see it as well in the progressive weakening of the will to exercise that authority along traditional lines. We can perceive it, too, in the excuses of prominent figures who attempt to justify illegal acts by pointing to the frequency with which they are committed.

It seems as if both the governed and the governors, the leaders and led, have let slip the moorings of the old morality and cast off in a current without benefit of compass or charts. They are searching for values, but the values perforce are empty because they have no links to the larger realities of community from which meaning, personal or otherwise, is ultimately derived.

Reasons for Moral Lapse

You can blame it on disenchantment with theology, a rejection of religion and with it the ethics and norms that religious authority has traditionally espoused. Or perhaps it is some primal hunger for a freedom that, once set loose, seeks to transcend not only the constraints of community but finitude itself—the godlike freedom celebrated in myth. It might even be, as many have claimed, the result of widespread affluence too quickly gained, a social manifestation of the axiom that "money buys freedom"—a freedom, unfortunately, that imitates license. Again, the moral lassitude may result from cultural commands like success and status, which have become accepted as absolutes that take precedence over principles and communal imperatives.

Watergate, viewed from the vantage of time, is but an acute manifestation of the underlying trends toward an amorality that continues to have a corrosive effect on our national life. The tendencies toward such amorality manifested themselves again with the disclosure that a substantial number of America's major corporations, in their dealings with foreign governments, have violated ethical and legal standards of both the United States and foreign countries. While some of these disclosures relate to actions taken prior to Watergate, other later ones demonstrate that crucial public lessons were lost upon the private sector.

An example is a statement of a management consultant quoted in *The Wall Street Journal*, who said that the congressional effort to curb improper foreign payments was spearheaded by "a bunch of pipsqueak moralists running around trying to apply U.S. puritanical standards to other countries." The Conference Board survey of business executives revealed that nearly half the executives questioned believed that their foreign operations should be governed by the ethical standards of the foreign host country and not those of the United States. Competitive considerations, they felt, should outweigh ethics.

This is a dangerously astigmatic outlook. The leadership role of the United States in the free world has been based in significant part on our willingness to set standards for our own conduct and that of others. If we relinquish our advocacy of such standards, we will pay, in the long term, a grave price. As pointed out by a perceptive Washington lawyer in regard to public disclosure of corporate venality: "Nothing we have recently done to ourselves has helped more to discredit private enterprise in both the U.S. and abroad—especially multinational private enterprise—and to speed the spread of the corporate state."

Questionable Payments Abroad

The multinational corporations have a particularly important role to play in the supply of capital and technology to less-developed countries. This productive relationship can, in an increasingly interdependent world, redound to the benefit of rich and poor nations alike. Exposure of the questionable payments problem has exacerbated concerns about multinationals' accountability to the national legal constraints of both home and foreign host countries. It has raised the level of concern that such enterprises have the capacity to conduct independent foreign policy, including the suborning of host country political and governmental processes. Increased anxiety regarding multinationals' legal and political accountability could lead to national and international "backlash" in the form of laws or regulations which could severely handicap such enterprises. The result could be seriously detrimental to the United States economy, to world commerce and to the pattern of world development.

Those who argue that the only full and fair means to stop questionable corporate payments abroad is a binding international agreement are right— beyond dispute. Such an agreement should be a strong diplomatic priority of this country. But the process of negotiating such an agreement will be long and difficult. The prospects are uncertain. In the meantime, we should take unilateral steps to restore confidence in U.S. business entities, regardless of possible competitive consequences. In so doing, we as the world's foremost economic power, and the chief progenitor of multinational corporations will set an example for our trading partners.

Legislative Proposal

As a means of dealing with this problem, the cabinet-level Task Force on Questionable Corporate Payments Abroad, of which I was chairman, recommended a reporting system in which all U.S. businesses would be required to report to the Secretary of Commerce certain classes of payments, together with names of recipients, made by such firms and their 50-percent-owned foreign subsidiaries. These reports would subsequently be made available to the public.

This approach takes into account that sunlight is a potent disinfectant, as Justice Brandeis noted; or as H.L. Mencken once observed, "Conscience is the inner voice that warns us somebody may be looking."

The proposed legislation's systematic reporting requirements and public disclosure of the reports' contents were designed to help build public confidence in U.S. business. It would make dealings with foreign governments take place in the open. The reports would be transferred to appropriate foreign agencies by the Attorney General or the Secretary of State. In this fashion, they would serve as a goad to foreign governments to enforce their own laws, since nearly every nation in the world has laws against public bribery and extortion.

The task force felt that the "sunlight" approach was more enforceable than a direct criminal statute since it eschews need of proof of the intent of the payor at the time payments are made. While not seeking unilaterally under U.S. law to criminalize foreign improper payments, the proposed legislation did contain definite criminal penalties for negligent or willful failure to report or for falsification or omission of information in reports.

We cannot delude ourselves, however, that the law, by itself, will suffice. We must recognize the validity of the observation that "law reflects but in no sense determines the moral worth of a society." The law can define standards of behavior that are morally and ethically right, but it cannot make that behavior a reality.

Whatever the cause of our disintegrating moral consensus, one thing is certain: Without the precepts of morality to guide behavior, it is impossible to mediate the competing claims of individuals in a free society—especially, and most particularly, the fundamental and far-reaching claims of liberty and equality, as well as those of individuality.

We have to establish a balance between the claims of liberty and equality—

between liberty and equality among individuals demanding more of both in a society that can only allow, with justice and order, so much of each. In the final analysis, liberty and equality are moral values that rest on the obligation to respect other human beings. They entail the duty not merely to resist incursions and infringements of rights, but to desist in making claims on others when it becomes apparent that your liberty or your equality or your self-fulfillment can only be achieved at the expense of others.

The precepts of the old morality may seem irrelevant as the communities that uphold them disappear, swallowed up by urbanization, flattened out by uniformity, overwhelmed by complexity, diminished by distant bureaucracy, exhausted by the mobility of their inhabitants. They may seem irrelevant to rootless individuals lacking in emotional attachment to a society that is indifferent to them, trapped in a world of ego-centered desires and gratifications. Ceasing to believe in the reality of other people, and with no capacity for empathy, we can cheat them, steal from them and hurt them with no fellow-feeling for their loss or pain.

No one knows for sure why crime in the United States has increased so alarmingly in recent decades. But nearly five years of involvement with the problems of criminal justice have convinced me that the increase is directly proportionate to the decline of community—and the weakening of the old morality that follows from it.

The old morality calls for self-discipline—and that is why, in a free society, it can never be irrelevant. For if we dismiss the relevance of self-restraint, we invite an ever more pervasive restraint of law, and an ever more permeative encroachment of law on liberty and individuality.

3-4 Multinational Corporations and East Asia: The Foreign Policy Implications of the Lockheed Affair*

Frank Church

On August 20, 1972, A.C. Kotchian, president of the Lockheed Corporation, checked into a suite on the tenth floor of the Hotel Okura in Tokyo, and set in train the events which were to lead to the biggest scandal in the postwar history of Japan; his own dismissal along with that of Daniel Haughton, chairman of the board of Lockheed; and the most profound reconsideration in the United States of corporate morality, power and influence since the Teapot Dome scandal of the early 1920s. But the Lockheed affair, as it has unfolded on a worldwide stage, is more than a corporate immorality play. It is a disturbing illustration of the extent to which basic assumptions about the American economy and international politics have become outmoded.

*Speech at Harvard East Asia Conference, October 15, 1976.

What I want to discuss with you today are some of the implications for American foreign policy of the Lockheed story which have not been generally commented upon.

Kotchian's Mission

When Mr. Kotchian arrived in Japan on that August day in 1972, his mission was nothing less than to save the Lockheed Corporation from impending bankruptcy. The company was then, and is now, the largest defense contractor in the United States. (Corporate sales in 1975 amounted to an estimated $3.5 billion.) But in the late 1960s, Lockheed's management had made a major decision to diversify its business and compete with Boeing and McDonnell-Douglas in the manufacture and sale of commercial airliners. Lockheed had thus developed the L-1011 Tristar wide-bodied jumbo jet, but the program had misfired. Bankrolled by major U.S. banks to the tune of $650 million, the Tristar program threatened to drag the company into bankruptcy. By 1971, only a $250 million U.S. government guarantee of private bank loans enabled the company to survive. Lockheed's own projections showed that the company had to sell 300 of the jumbo jetliners in order for the program to break even. By 1972, however, the wide-bodied airline market appeared to be saturated; competition was fierce. Not only were the $250 million U.S. guaranteed loans in jeopardy, but another $400 million of unguaranteed loans from private banks were at serious risk.

The domestic U.S. market could not furnish the solution. The financial viability of the Tristar program ultimately depended upon Lockheed's success in selling the plan abroad. Furthermore, the success of the overseas sales effort increasingly appeared to depend upon Japan. For if the major Japanese international carrier, All Nippon Airlines, could be persuaded to purchase the Tristar, it would not only be a major sale—21 planes in all were sold for nearly $400 million—but it would be a prestige sale, placing the Tristar on a par with Boeing's 747 and McDonnell-Douglas' DC 10. As seen by the Lockheed management, Japan was not a market which they could afford to lose.

In effect, then, the solvency of the leading American defense contractor rested upon its ability to accomplish a sale in the international market of civilian aircraft. The Lockheed case dramatically illustrates the fact that critical elements of the American economy have outgrown the geographical confines of the United States. The aerospace industry can no longer be economically defined in terms of the American market. Its sales effort, to succeed, must be international in scope: in Lockheed's case, its 60,000 jobs, $650 million in private bank financing, $250 million in U.S. government-backed guarantees, all seemingly hinged upon the success or failure of selling the Tristar to the Japanese.

The issue, then, for the United States is not whether it should be, or wishes to be, part of this world market. Rather, it is the terms upon which we are to participate in it. What we have failed to realize is that those terms are today defined, to a very large degree, by the corporations seeking sales abroad.

Lockheed as Political Actor

What precisely did Mr. Kotchian do when he set up his command post in the Okura Hotel? In a remarkable five-part interview in the Asahai Evening News, he outlined the Lockheed sales campaign in detail. The crux of the problem for Lockheed was to persuade All Nippon Airlines to postpone a decision to buy the McDonnell-Douglas DC 10, and then arrange for All Nippon to buy the Lockheed Tristar, instead. In order to accomplish this objective, Kotchian undertook to penetrate the very top level of Japanese political decision making. He enlisted the aid of Lockheed's secret agent in Japan, Yoshio Kodama, a leader of the ultra-right-wing nationalist faction of Japanese politics, a man with close ties to conservative elements of the Japanese ruling party, an unsavory figure who had served three years in Sugamo prison at the end of World War II as a suspected class A war criminal, an individual with known ties to the Japanese underworld. For his services in promoting the Tristar sale, as well as for other services rendered, Kodama received from Lockheed approximately $7 million. The disposition of these funds as of this date is not yet known.

According to Kotchian's sworn testimony before the Multinational Subcommittee, Lockheed also dispatched $2 million through other channels to Japanese government officials in order to ensure that the "right" decisions were made. In effect, Lockheed, in pursuing its commercial interests, had become a nefarious political actor in Japan. It had secretly retained Kodama as its sales agent, a leader of that political faction in Japan which the United States government had regarded, since the close of World War II, as inimical to our national interests. And in making payoffs to various politicians in the Japanese government, the company contributed to the corruption and subversion of the ruling party, on which the United States heavily relied. To say that Lockheed was merely promoting the sale of its product and did not consciously intend any mischief, is equivalent to saying that a man who lets a bull loose in a china shop simply intends for it to browse, not to break any china!

The lesson of the Lockheed case, then, is that an American multinational corporation can become a political actor abroad whose immediate interests may be antithetical to the foreign policy objectives of the United States. Nor is Lockheed an isolated case. In the course of our three-year investigation, we found the ITT Corporation attempting to subvert the electoral processes of Chile; the Gulf Oil Corporation making $4 million in illegal political contributions to General Park's party in Korea; and in Italy, a concerted plan by the major oil companies for multimillion dollar payments to Italian political parties in return for legislative favors. We can no longer pretend that what these corporations do abroad is strictly their own business and of little interest or concern to the government of the United States.

I do not ignore that some of these corporations, as in the case of ITT in Chile, acted with the encouragement of government agencies, like the CIA. But more often, as in the cases of Japan, Korea and Italy, the subcommittee has been told by the responsible U.S. government officials that they had no knowledge of the political payments, bribes or questionable commission fees disclosed by the subcommittee. It could be that these are disingenuous denials designed to conceal the background role of our own government in such gross misconduct. But I think it is more likely that the disclaimers reflect the traditional attitude of our diplomats that commercial activities abroad of American-owned corporations are simply none of their business. Such an attitude betrays a failure to understand that multinational corporations often are crucial actors in the international political sphere, whose activities may determine and define U.S. national interests to a degree comparable to the actions of our own government.

The most recent evidence of this tendency is to be found in the subcommittee's investigation of the arms trade in the Persian Gulf. Here, it was clearly demonstrated, in the case of Grumman's sale of F-14 fighter planes to Iran, that long before the U.S. government made any decision to permit the sale abroad of this advanced aircraft, Grumman had effectively promoted its sale at the highest levels of the Iranian government. Confronted with the insistent demands of the Shah for the F-14, the U.S. government's "decision" to allow the sale was, in reality, a mere ratification of a deal already concluded—for all practical purposes—between the manufacturer and the customer government, a deal much too far advanced to be called off without the most serious repercussions. In these circumstances, one must ask who is effectively determining national policy, the corporate salesmen or the U.S. government?

Traditional diffidence where private business is concerned may account for the tardy recognition by our diplomats of this new reality in international politics. If they persist in viewing the commercial solicitations of our largest corporations as somewhat irrelevant to their work, they will discover too late that important decisions, involving our national interests, have effectively been taken from their hands.

The Subcommittee Investigation

But it is not only the diplomatic establishment which has to change traditional attitudes. The Lockheed scandal presented dilemmas for the Congress as well. The Senate subcommittee, which I chaired, was charged with investigating the global role of multinational corporations and its impact on our foreign policy. Lockheed's misconduct, if revealed, might severely strain relations with Japan. Yet, Lockheed's payoffs, and those of Northrop, Exxon, Gulf and others, convinced the subcommittee that legislation was essential if the wrongs we discovered were to be effectively inhibited. In order to provide a basis and secure the necessary support for legislation, the subcommittee concluded, in the Lockheed case, as with Gulf, Northrop, and Exxon, that public hearings were mandatory.

But it was also apparent that disclosure of such widespread bribery abroad could disrupt many a government—including such frontline allies as Japan, the Netherlands, and Italy, as well as certain key governments in the Middle East. We had to reconcile the need for obtaining public and congressional support for remedial legislation with a recognition that the foreign government potentially involved must be treated with fairness and restraint.

In the Japanese case, Lockheed's intention to pay government officials in order to advance the sale of the Tristar was clear from the sworn testimony and documentary record in the subcommittee's possession. But because of the absence of incontrovertible proof that payments had actually been received by the intended officials, the subcommittee had to proceed with caution. Special procedures were devised.

From the beginning of the inquiry, the subcommittee had adopted the view that maximum public disclosure would be the rule, but that it would not reveal the names of foreign government officials accused of receiving the money. However, the identity of the country in which the payments were made would be disclosed. If the foreign government wished to pursue the matter, the subcommittee stood willing to cooperate. But, since a congressional committee should not deal directly with a foreign government, we decided to transmit requested documents and testimony through the Department of State. In the Lockheed case, the subcommittee specifically informed then Under Secretary Robert Ingersoll, a former U.S. Ambassador to Japan, that it intended to reveal in public hearings the identity of Kodama, Lockheed's secret agent in Japan, as well as the fact that certain unnamed Japanese government officials were alleged to have received payments. Ingersoll stated that the Department of State had no objection to these disclosures and did not wish to be heard on the subject.

The subcommittee proceeded with public hearings on February 4 and 6; Mr. Kotchian testified to payments by Lockheed to Kodama and Japanese government officials, as well as payments intended for high government officials in the Netherlands and Italy. In line with its policy, the subcommittee did not make public the names of the intended recipients. But, on the request of Japan and the other governments involved, the evidence in the subcommittee's possession was transferred to the State Department which used as its agent in negotiating with the foreign governments the Department of Justice.

The results, I think, have been impressive. Reacting to the disclosures in the Lockheed hearings, Congress passed a Foreign Military Sales Bill, which incorporated provisions Senator Percy and I authored requiring public disclosure of all commissions, fees and other payments to foreign agents engaged in promoting the sale of arms. In addition, the Senate passed a bill sponsored by Senator Proxmire making the payment of a bribe abroad a crime under U.S. law. Although Congress adjourned before the House had an opportunity to consider the bill, it seems certain of passage in the next session. Moreover, the New York Stock Exchange has proposed a requirement that listed companies have audit committees composed of outside directors to review, among other matters, questionable overseas payments, a proposal which *The Wall Street Journal* in an astonishing editorial, implied was Marxist, when Senators Pearson, Clark and I first proposed it.

In the Japanese case, fears were expressed that disclosure of Lockheed's misconduct in that country would endanger its internal political stability and longstanding friendship with the United States. But this paternalistic view underestimated the vitality of Japanese democracy. As a well-known columnist wrote recently:

... when Lockheed surfaced there was a school at the State Department that sought to suppress, or at least muffle, the scandal. The belief was that Japan could not take an exportation of American morality without falling back into the bad old ways.
In fact, nothing of the sort has occurred. The Japanese have handled the prosecution in a careful way. Newspapers and TV have done their stuff as guardians of the national morality. The public opinion polls show that ordinary people support the governments' effort to get at the truth. There have even been moves toward writing a new campaign finance law.

Let me close with a final reflection upon the Lockheed affair. What I have tried to describe to you is the way in which the Lockheed case illustrates a web of entanglement: a major U.S. defense contractor seeks its financial salvation in sales abroad; it penetrates and corrupts the internal politics of major allies of the United States, our own government admits that this fraudulent and corrosive behavior has taken place outside its knowledge and control; and, when a congressional committee proposes to expose the sordid facts and legislate to prevent their repetition, we are told that to do so would endanger the security of the United States.

The Lockheed case was, indeed, a sensation, more so in Japan and Western Europe than in the United States. We *do* live in an interdependent world. But that is no reason to tread lightly in cleaning up the corrupt practices of multinational corporations. There is every indication that instead of incurring the animosity of other peoples, our investigation, disclosure and enactment of remedial legislation engendered admiration abroad. Japan, the Netherlands and others opened their own investigations based upon the initial disclosures of our subcommittee. The results have not been destructive, but regenerative, for nothing saps the confidence of people in their government more than the conviction that official corruption is a way of life, never to be revealed or remedied. The Lockheed case tells us that the international community is far more durable and mature than some would have us believe, and that America does best when it follows its own best instincts.

3-5 Ethical Perspectives on Business and Society

Roderick M. Hills

During my first year as chairman of the Securities and Exchange Commission, I have been deeply involved in the ongoing investigations of some of this nation's largest corporations for illegal and unethical corporate payments. However, before detailing the trouble spots in the business community, my basic conclusions are:

> That some improvement in corporate behavior is now underway,
>
> That we should make only a few precise changes in the law,
>
> That we should pay more attention to enforcing the laws already on the books, but
>
> That we should not overreact to this whole chapter of corporate history.

My own perspective of what is primarily wrong with our large corporations does not call for major new federal legislation. Rather, it seeks a reorientation of existing agencies and organizations to continue a long and concentrated effort to change the manner in which our corporations are managed.

First, the subject is divisible into three simplistic parts:

1. Corporate behavior that is contrary to law
2. Corporate behavior that is contrary to good business practices
3. Corporate behavior that is contrary to someone's notion of good public policy

Contrary to Law

We do know that over 300 companies have made questionable or illegal payments in the U.S. or abroad, and the commission has prosecuted over a score of major cases to consent decrees. The result in each case has been to secure both a purging of past misbehavior and a change in the governance of the corporation to be reasonably sure that such misbehavior will not be repeated.

We conclude as a commission that we have adequate remedies with which to deal with concealed questionable payments, but we have suggested changes in the law which would put more pressure on management and the accounting profession to keep better records and public pressure on the New York Stock Exchange to give far more responsibility to outside directors. Our efforts under existing law and our request for new laws are to create an internal reporting system that will place these rather difficult payment questions squarely before the independent directors, outside auditors and outside counsel.

Contrary to Good Management Practices

Much can be done to improve management practices to achieve both a more profitable company and a greater responsiveness to ethical concerns:

> Too many boards are dominated by inside directors. Even where there are significant numbers of outsiders on a board, they are all too often old friends of the chief executive officer, who would rather resign from the board than severely criticize or vote to oust their old friend.
>
> Compensation for directors of too many large corporations is set at a figure which makes it apparent that no real work is expected.
>
> Information provided to boards of directors in too many cases is entirely the product of management, and no effort is made and no authority is given to outside directors to make an independent investigation.
>
> Inside directors vote too often on salaries of employees, on questions of whether merger proposals should be accepted or on tender offers—all subjects that present conflict of interest to management.

Directors seldom turn ineffective management out. As a result, stockholder democracy in most cases means simply the right to sell the stock.

Companies limp along under poor management until either economic setbacks are so severe that change is compelled or until a large perceptive investor or company bids for stock control, recognizing that the corporate assets can produce better profits. Management is too often complacent, self-perpetuating and unresponsive to legitimate shareholders' demands. When reported profits decline to such an extent as to threaten the serenity of their well-paid isolation, some managers are tempted to change the accounting practices, the earnings figures, or the morals of their company in order to present a more pleasing profit picture.

Proposals for Reform

What is missing on too many boards is a truly independent force that has the practical capacity to monitor and to change management. However, one must declare strongly that what is missing on some boards is present on others. We do have splendidly performing companies that have effective, responsive, and responsible boards of directors.

As we look for solutions, it seems more sensible to recast the poorly performing boards according to the model of the successful companies than to experiment with a totally new system of corporate governance. The essential first step is the creation of a panel of outside directors that will meet privately with the outside auditors. Directors must be paid more and must spend more time on corporate business. The independent members of the board must have some automatic method to secure information about operations. The independent board members must also create some objective criteria of performance for management. Finally, the independent board member must have exclusive jurisdiction to approve or veto decisions on certain types of issues such as salaries, merger proposals, and selection of auditors, and the repurchase of corporate stock.

The trend is quite promising. One survey shows that in less than five years the number of corporations with independent audit committees jumped from under 50% to almost 90%. Moreover, the New York Stock Exchange has recently adopted a proposal providing that independent audit committees with true authority be established and maintained as a requirement for listing on the Exchange. This change will greatly encourage corporate accountability among members of the Exchange. We also know that there are many other major corporations experimenting with the role to be played by their boards. We can reasonably assume, therefore, that a better system of management accountability is coming.

Federal Chartering

Although some have suggested that corporate behavior be reformed by a federal corporation law, I do not believe that federal chartering will really help maintain more lawful corporate behavior. It is equally apparent, I feel, that federal chartering will not bring about better-managed companies. The final question is whether we want corporations to have an independent duty to be responsive to public policy. Should they be instrumentalities of public policies that are not set forth in statute?

It is tempting to put public interest directors on a board to speak for employees, for environment, for a better life! It is admittedly difficult for Congress to strike a balance between needed economic growth and environmental improvement—between the need for profits and the desire for safe products and working conditions. The temptation may be great to transfer these problems to boards and make them get board members who have the broader public interest at heart.

My simple response to this suggestion is that it will not work. In a discussion of the evolution of similar considerations in Europe it has been noted:

Public policy had been parcelled out among committees, organizations and enterprises throughout the society ... and the result ... has been a growing tendency to use large national enterprises to solve specific problems as if they were agencies of the state. And, there has been a related tendency to develop methods of government that have reduced the role of the parliamentary process and elevated the role of specialized groups.

In sum, when governments have tried to make corporations instruments of government policy, the corporations become less efficient and the governments become less democratic.

My view of business in the U.S. today is that, while many major companies have failed their stockholders and the public, many more have devised methods of governance that make their management truly accountable to independent directors who are responsible. Our effort should be to raise the standard of business leaders to that of those who are doing the job well. Only if we fail to make steady progress should we force a greater federal intrusion into business management.

I confess a great concern for the sometimes strident but always impatient call for change now! I also confess a great affection for words written by a San Francisco longshoreman in the 1960s:

If one were to pick the chief trait which characterizes the temper of our time, it would be impatience. Tomorrow has become a dirty word. The future is now, and hope has turned into desire. ... The better part of statesmanship might be to know clearly and precisely what not to do, and leave action to the improvisation of chance.

The "chance" of Watergate gave us a better government and began a series of corporate investigations that has already improved our vision and raised corporate behavioral standards. I suggest a steady and cautious course as we pursue further improvements, to avoid needlessly interfering with the capacity of our business community to maintain innovative growth. At stake are not merely the profits of business, but the economic freedom upon which our form of democracy is dependent.

**Part II
Business and Society**

Introduction to Part II

The dilemma faced by the business community in connection with its responsibility toward society is the age-old dichotomy between economics and ethics. As Albert Carr queries, "Can an executive afford a conscience?"[1] In the article "Is Ethics Good Business?" Yerachmiel Kugel and Gladys W. Gruenberg set forth the framework within which this issue has been discussed in the past and attempt to resolve the dilemma, suggesting that whatever reform is needed can serve not only to reinforce the free market system, but also to support the individual executive's own moral code. They conclude that the long-run interest of society is not incompatible with long-run interests of business and the individual executive.

While some critics decry business' pursuit of self-interest at the expense of morality and the good of the community, others would condemn business as a corrupting influence on society. A typical example of this attitude is seen in the argument advanced by Nader and Green.[2] Irving Kristol, on the other hand, attributes business criticism to the lack of effective economic education. He calls upon the business community to lead the way in presenting economic reality in such a way as to eradicate misconceptions about business goals and conduct.

As an indication of the fact that business is far from voiceless, we have assembled a sample of responses from business executives themselves. William H. Wendel of The Carborundum Company clearly points out the dimensions of the problem, coloring business ethics in many shades of gray. W. Michael Blumenthal, Secretary of the Treasury, formerly Chairman of Bendix Corporation, suggests a solution in the form of an international association of business executives to police industry ethical standards, while Frank T. Cary of IBM stresses the role of business leadership and insists that the first line of attack is the corporate code of ethics and the moral leadership of the chief executive officer.

Irving S. Shapiro of Du Pont, current chairman of The Business Roundtable, sounds a somewhat different note, coming out strongly against business immorality but warning that nit-picking in this area can be counterproductive. He emphasizes the role of an improved board of directors in providing moral leadership and feels that business is capable of instituting its own reforms, urging immediate action by powerful business organizations and multinational firms.

Discussion of the propriety of business actions inevitably turns to the larger question of business social responsibility and how business goals and societal goals interact. To what extent is the present economic system responsible for the moral dilemma business faces? Albert Levi concludes that business ethical conduct may be impossible without professionalizing the business community. He is not too optimistic about accomplishing that goal because of competitive pressures.

Donald E. Schwartz of Georgetown Law Center implies that implementation of reform should be confined to the present economic system. Schwartz would improve the firm's decision-making process by making it more responsive to societal needs in three major areas: (1) shareholder voting machinery, (2) corporate self-criticism, and (3) data disclosure.

Expanding on the ethical influences which face businessmen, Robert Henle, S.J., emphasizes the roles of family, church, and education as institutional subsystems to create a "just" people leading to a better system.

All of the contributors in Part II are serious students of the business community and the ethical dilemma. What they have to say will undoubtedly shape the form and substance of society's response.

Notes

1. Albert Z. Carr, "Can an Executive Afford a Conscience?" *Harvard Business Review* (July-August 1970), pp. 58-74; reprinted in Kugel and Gruenberg, *Selected Readings on International Payoffs.*

2. Cf. Ralph Nader and Mark Green, "What To Do About Corporate Corruption," *The Wall Street Journal*, March 12, 1976; Arthur Schlesinger, Jr., "Government, Business and Morality," *The Wall Street Journal*, June 1, 1976.

4 The Ethical Debate

4-1 Is Ethics Good Business?

Yerachmiel Kugel and **Gladys W. Gruenberg**

In this article we attempt to account for the wide range of answers to the title question. Why is it that business executives are quite evenly divided on whether the answer should be yes or no? To understand the ethical considerations of the businessman, it is necessary to assess the influences which shape his general beliefs and values. Many studies have been made to illustrate and analyze the experience of business executives with ethical questions.[1] We have set forth the results of these studies elsewhere[2] and do not intend to repeat that analysis here. However, some general conclusions are in order.

Listed among the most influential factors in determination of personal goals and aspirations among businessmen are the following:

1. Family and personal considerations
2. Company policy and peer group standards
3. Educational background and religious training

Competition in the industry is the overriding business reason for unethical behavior. Exemplification of this belief is Albert Carr's comparison of business decision making to a poker game.[3] Like poker players businessmen are expected to seize any opportunity to win so long as it does not involve outright cheating. Bluffing, for instance, is not only permissible, but respected if done successfully.

Competition in the industry has been likened to warfare, justifying the ethical rules of self-defense. However, Thomas Garrett, S.J., notes that such ethics "demand that the attack be unjust and that all normal means of defense, such as the courts, should have been tried before extreme (unethical?) measures are taken."[4] The view that business practice must be ethical regardless of mitigating circumstances holds that competition (the "everybody else doing it" argument) does not justify unethical practices. For instance, if a business firm controlled by the underworld uses criminal practices to achieve its goals, does that justify an ordinary businessman in following suit to meet such competition?[5]

As a well-known code of ethics states: "The law is a floor. Ethical business conduct should normally exist at a level well above the minimum required by law."[6] Such a precept insures business against "economic Darwinism"[7] and the rapid deterioration of the environment in which business operates.

Our investigation of international payoffs reveals that the type of industry and market, and the economic relationship with the host country, have a great deal to do with a firm's attitude toward business ethics, and that it may vary depending on the local environment.[8]

United Brands, for example, undoubtedly felt that ethics was not good business in Honduras when its banana shipments became jeopardized by a threatened doubling of the export tax. Lockheed winked at ethics when its sales of aircraft in Japan became dependent on bribes to various government officials responsible for making purchase decisions both for defense and private air transportation. Gulf acceded to unethical conduct in South Korea to protect a multimillion dollar investment in petrochemical and fertilizer plants. All of these threats add up to increased costs or reduction of benefits, causing company executives to place economics ahead of ethics.

In summary, these studies imply that there are various alternatives available to the business executive in determining whether or not ethics is good business. They can be reduced to one basic question: Do the benefits outweigh the costs? Those who insist that ethics is good business are sure that morality pays and that costs outweigh benefits in the long run. Those who condone unethical conduct in the name of business economics are equally adamant in their contention that ethical behavior may not be compatible with business viability in certain markets where specific economic elements create a climate for unethical activities.

It is our belief that the cost-benefit ratio can be swung firmly to the side of ethical behavior by increasing the incentives for moral conduct and the disincentives for immoral conduct on the part of individual executives charged with business decision making. Foremost among disincentives is the increased chance of disclosure and penalty. Incentives involve increased stature in the public eye for those business executives who become noted for ethical judgment and who speak out forcefully in behalf of legislation to censure those business actions which society deems unethical. Social pressure in the form of law enforcement and prosecution for white-collar crimes[9] stands high on the list of disincentives to convince business executives that ethics is good business, good for them as individuals and good for the firm which employs them. Their long-run self-interest must be equated with the long-run self-interest of society. This can be done only through specifically designed legislation aimed at the individual executive.

Table 4-1 gives a run-down of the specific questions which individual executives should ask to arrive at their ethical cost-benefit calculation in connection with specific business decisions. This calculation gives the answer to the question: Is ethics good business?[10]

Table 4-1
Cost-benefit (c-b) Checklist for Ethical Decision Making

No. and Type	Questions to be Answered	1 For Action	2 Uncertain	3 Against Action
A. Legal				
1.	What are the legal consequences?	Light	Fair	Severe
2.	How comprehensive is the law? What is the enforceability of law?	Limited	Somewhat extensive	Very extensive
3.	Can the justice system be influenced?	Yes	Maybe	No
4.	Will the corporation be liable to its competitors for financial damages (such as unfair practice, restraint of trade)?	Very unlikely	Possible	Probable
5.	Will the company be held liable by stockholders?	Very unlikely	Possible	Probable
B. Moral				
1.	What is the company's policy? (Will it cause any deviation from standard practice?)	Acceptable	If necessary	Unacceptable
2.	If the questionable action is disclosed, will it damage the public image of the company?	Slightly	Somewhat	Seriously
3.	Will the activity affect employee morale of the company?	No	Maybe	Yes
4.	What is the custom?	Acceptable practice	Illegal, but everyone does it	Absolutely prohibited
5.	Does the public opinion carry weight?	No	Depends	Yes

Table 4-1 (cont.)

No. and Type	Questions to be Answered	1 For Action	2 Uncertain	3 Against Action
C. Economic				
1.	How does the expected gain compare with the company's total earnings?	High	Medium	Low
2.	What is the cost as a percentage of total revenue? Is it one-time or periodic?	High	Fair	Low
3.	Is the company diversified?	Yes	Somewhat	No
4.	Will the action trigger others to make the same demand?	Very unlikely	Maybe	Very likely
5.	Will the action cause retaliation from competitors?	They started it	Possible	Yes
D. Personal				
1.	Will top management find out? If so, am I subject to censure?	Very unlikely	Maybe	Very likely
2.	Am I likely to be held personally liable for such action?	Very unlikely	Possible	Probable
3.	Does the company carry insurance to pay my legal fees if I am found guilty of violating a law?	Yes	Uncertain	No
4.	Will disclosure harm my reputation and make it difficult to obtain or retain a management position in the future?	Very unlikely	Maybe	Very likely
5.	How would my family and friends react to disclosure of such activity?	Approve	Indifferent	Disapprove

TOTAL NUMBER OF BOXES CHECKED

THE c-b INDICATOR*

Source: Adapted from Yerachmiel Kugel and Gladys W. Gruenberg, *International Payoffs: Dilemma for Business*, (Lexington, Mass.: Lexington Books, D.C. Heath and Company, 1977), chapter 6.

Instructions for Use of Checklist

To arrive at the c-b indicator:

1. Add the total number of boxes checked.

2. Assume all the answers carry equal weight:
   Use 1 x (no. in column 1) + 0 x (no. in column 2) + (–1) x (no. in column 3) = c-b indicator.

3. Assign a different weight to each question as desired:
   Use 1 x (total weight of column 1) + 0 x (total weight of column 2) + (–1) x (total weight of column 3) = c-b indicator.

Interpretation of the c-b indicator:

1. Positive—At least the gain is greater than the risk. The higher the total, the less important risks become.

2. Zero—The gain and risk are fifty-fifty.

3. Negative—The gain is outweighed by the risks.

Notes

1. The two classics in this field are John W. Clark, S.J., *Religion and the Moral Standards of American Businessmen* (Cincinnati: South-Western Publishing Co., 1966) and Raymond Baumhart, S.J., *An Honest Profit* (New York: Holt, Rinehart and Winston, 1968). Other studies include the American Management Association's *The Changing Success Ethic* (New York: AMACOM, 1973); Archie Carroll, "A Survey of Managerial Ethics: Is Business Morality Watergate Morality?" *Business and Society Review* (Spring 1975), pp. 58-60; "Business Executives and Moral Dilemmas," a *Business and Society Review* survey, *Business and Society Review* (Spring 1975), pp. 51-57.

2. Kugel and Gruenberg, *International Payoffs: Dilemma for Business*, Chapter 3.

3. Albert Z. Carr, "Is Business Bluffing Ethical?" *Harvard Business Review* (January-February 1968), pp. 143-153.

4. Thomas Garrett, S.J., *Business Ethics* (New York: Appleton-Century Crofts, 1966), p. 98.

5. Cf. *The Wall Street Journal*, March 3, 1977, account of the "Brooklyn Cheese Mafia."

6. Caterpillar Tractor Co., *A Code of Worldwide Business Conduct*, reprinted in Kugel and Gruenberg, *Selected Readings on International Payoffs*.

7. Leo C. Brown, S.J., "Marxism," *New Catholic Encyclopedia* (New York: McGraw-Hill Book Co., 1967), vo. IX, p. 335.

8. Cf. Kugel and Gruenberg, *International Payoffs: Dilemma for Business*, Chapter 4.

9. Ibid., Chapter 7.

10. In the aftermath of the international payoff scandal, reports show that the crackdown on international bribery has not damaged sales, and reform has not reduced profits for companies that have instituted widespread disclosure and corporate controls to prevent recurrence of such activities in the future. Cf. *The Wall Street Journal*, January 25, and February 28, 1977.

4-3 Business Faces Critics' Challenge*

Irving Kristol

Every now and then a pollster will report on the condition of economic literacy in this country, and his findings are always the same: the situation is deplorable. The average American has the most fanciful ideas on how much money a

---
*Commitment (Summer 1976), pp. 1, 8. (Abbott Laboratories, Chicago, Illinois.) Reprinted with permission.

corporation makes on each sale of its product, how much of corporate income goes to the government in taxes, what the costs of pensions, social security, unemployment insurance, etc., are to the corporation, and so on. In general, Americans grossly overestimate the affluence of corporations, seem blithely unaware that "profits" are merely retained earnings which are invested in new plants, new processes, new jobs, and seem strangely unconcerned about the economic vitality of our major economic institutions.

Naturally, businessmen get very upset when they read these findings and begin to think furiously about the need for "economic education." Now, it must be said that economic education—like practically all forms of education—is a good thing in itself. The more the American people understand economics, the more realistic will be their appraisal of various economic policies, the less vulnerable they will be to a political demagogy which exploits their misconceptions. It must also be said that corporations have, on the whole, been negligent of their responsibilities in this area. Only a few corporations, for instance, have well-organized, interesting classes in economics for their employees (*and* their wives or husbands). Similarly, very few corporations are even aware of the lamentable condition of economic education in elementary and high schools. So there is much work for the business community to do in the field of economic education, and it is time it set itself vigorously to this task.

Having said this, however, one must also go on to point out that there is more to "economic ignorance" than meets the eye. Indeed, the more carefully one contemplates this matter, the more complicated and bewildering it becomes.

For instance, one cannot help but wonder *why* "economic ignorance" should be so widespread today. After all, we are a far better-educated nation today than we were 50 years ago. A far greater percentage of our young people graduate from high school, far more go on to college. Moreover, our young people—and the population as a whole—read more magazines and books than ever was the case before. And yet, all this education seems to have been to little avail, so far as "economic ignorance" is concerned.

As a matter of fact, one has the impression that, if anything, there may have been *an increase* in "economic ignorance" over these past decades. Any high school or college teacher is quickly struck by the fact that young people today seem to have no clear understanding of how their parents go about making a living. This is the kind of knowledge that used to be absorbed as a matter of course in the home. Have parents stopped talking about it? Have children stopped listening? We don't know the answers to such questions, but we do know that the phenomenon itself is a very real one.

Moreover, it also appears to be the case that what we call common sense—the ability to observe the real world around one, and to make correct inferences from one's observations—is a less powerful mental faculty than it used to be. Thus, one hears students confidently assert that advertising on television "brainwashes" the viewer so that he ends up buying commodities he neither wants nor needs. But when one asks whether *they* have been so "brainwashed," or whether their own homes are full of such unwanted products, they are forced to reply in the negative. This lack of correspondence between what they *say* the world is like and what they *know* it to be like will disturb them, temporarily. Soon, however, they recover their equilibrium and proceed as if nothing had been learned. It is more than a little perplexing.

And most paradoxical of all, there is the fact that very well-educated people, of mature years, seem to be not much superior, so far as the conquest of "economic ignorance" is concerned, than their children or students. The extent of "economic ignorance" among college professors—including those who have taken their prescribed courses in economics—is utterly amazing. If one asks a group of academics about that hoary myth which claims that drug companies really have marvelous cures for all sorts of diseases but are suppressing such information to enhance their profits, a surprisingly large proportion will assert that there is certainly something to it. One would assume that learned men knew enough about the law governing drug patents, or about international competition in the drug industry, to dismiss such a paranoid fantasy—but one would assume wrong.

Now, when so many people know so much less than they ought to know, or could reasonably be expected to know, one begins to suspect that "economic ignorance" is only a part of the problem—and perhaps not the most important part. There are obviously powerful countervailing *emotions* at work here—emotions which obstruct and discourage the process of learning, whether in the classroom or in life.

One such emotion, especially among young people, is *fear.* The portrait of the businessman and the business community which these youngsters see on television or in the movies, or as presented in the books they read, is so villainous that these youngsters are scared silly at the prospect of entering the world of business (which most of them will of necessity do). Every professor who keeps in touch with his former students knows how astonished they all are when they discover, after graduation, that the world of business is really quite a decent and humane world after all—and that, in truth, they soon feel quite at home in it. But before this happens, it is their apprehensions that govern their attitudes, and it is out of such apprehension that a kind of *willful* "economic ignorance" emerges. They are so convinced that business is evil, are so disheartened at the thought of accommodating themselves to it, that they choose to interpret reality in ways unfavorable to it.

Another such emotion, especially among teachers and professors, is *competitive envy.* A teacher used to be someone who preferred a quiet and studious life to the strenuous life of business. (Remember Mr. Chips?) But with the tremendous expansion of education over the last 30 years, the teaching and academic professions are populated with many men and women who are "academic" only by courtesy of title, who are largely bored with academic routine, and who feel it is unjust that a successful entrepreneur or executive should make more money, or have a higher standing in the community, than they do. Inevitably, they pass on to their students, in all sorts of subtle ways, their basic attitude. With the contraction of the teaching profession now under way, this situation is improving somewhat. An academic career is becoming what it used to be: a matter of serious commitment, for which sacrifices are gladly made and accepted. Meanwhile, however, our educational institutions have too many men and women who stayed in schools all of their lives simply because it was the easiest and most comfortable thing to do—men and women who are by temperament "activist," who really belong in the world of business (or politics) but are "stuck" in an academic career. Out of their resentment there springs a hostility to the business community which takes many forms, one of them being a willful "economic ignorance."

And then, of course, there are the "intellectuals"—the men and women who write our books, make our TV shows and movies, edit our magazines, etc. These people always have conceived of themselves as constituting a kind of secular theocracy, and have consequently disliked a democratic business community for being insufficiently respectful of their talents and moral authority. This class creates the culture when permeates our society—and it is decidedly and obviously an anti-business culture. When was the last time you read a novel, or saw a movie, in which an honest businessman was the hero?

So the overcoming of "economic ignorance," if that is ever to take place, will have to involve much more than "economic education" in the conventional sense. There are vast cultural dimensions to this problem, and it is in precisely those dimensions that business executives feel least at home. But, if our liberal democracy is to survive, business executives are going to have to start exploring these unfamiliar worlds, and coping with the odd creatures they will discover there. They will experience many strange adventures, some quite hair-raising. But they are used to taking risks, are not easily intimidated, and in any case have no choice. Their very survival as free men—and our survival as a free nation—depends on the conquest and settlement of these wild and unruly regions.

5

Business' Response

5-1 Ethics—The Many Shades of Gray*

William H. Wendel

When I was asked to make this talk, the subject suggested was social responsibility. Later, after deciding I had the temerity to talk about ethics, I asked if I could change the subject. It was a foolish question. After I thought through what I wanted to say, it was abundantly clear that the subject had not changed. The fact is that without ethics and morals, there can be no social responsibility. Any effort at social consciousness without high moral principles is a sham, a deception.

I say this positively, even though I and a great many others have difficulty in defining ethics. Webster's says it is "the discipline dealing with what is good or bad." Not nearly as explicit as the story about the boy who asked his father, "Dad, what is ethics?" The reply was, "If a customer comes into my store and pays me $10 too much, the question is: should I tell my partner? That's ethics."

"What is ethics" is the subject, next to inflation and unemployment, receiving the most attention in the general and business press today—not capital formation or exchange rates or balance of payments, but scandal, business scandal. Perhaps scandal is always the favorite of the press. Most of what I read was sensational rather than analytical, so I decided to take a crack at analysis. I also checked with a friend well known to this group. He said that purchasing people are on the leading edge of business ethical questions and from the literature he sent me, I learned this has been part of the deliberations of this organization and its predecessor for many years. I will try to take a different tack, however, from those who addressed you in the past.

My thesis is that ethics and morality are a function of both time and place. Further, the rate of change in ethics and morals, like the rate of change in every other aspect of our society, is increasing. Some observers go further and say that "our old definitions of values are wasting away and new ones are appearing, however obscurely. Such basic tenets as individualism, private property, a weak central government are assuming the status of discarded totems. The purposes and priorities of our society are not clear. We as managers can no longer rely on old notions of what is right but must try to assess what is going to be right in the future."

---
*Speech before Chemical Buyers Group, Purchasing Management Association, October 16, 1975.

Before trying to look to the future, let's look briefly at the past. That ethics depend on time can be dramatically illustrated. After the Civil War, right here in upper New York State, the building of the railroads involved bribery of cabinet members, judges, and state legislators; watered stock; falsification of corporate records; conspiracy to fix rates; extortion by refusing to move freight; assault, and theft. Famous names were involved—Drew, Fisk, and Gould. Remarkably, much of the public reaction was one of a huge entertainment.

In Pennsylvania, another famous name, Carnegie, broke contracts when demand for steel was high, in order to raise prices on the new orders. He paid commissions to railroad purchasing agents, and won secret rebates from the railroads for shipping steel over their lines. In Ohio, Rockefeller established an oil combine by buying out his competitors under threat of bankruptcy to force special rates from the railroads, control output, dictate prices, and conduct espionage. Later, the industry was involved in theft, arson, and slaughter.

Further west, the meat packers formed a combine to eliminate competition for supply, broke worker strikes by a system of blacklisting and set their own sanitary rules so liberally that the owners did not eat their own processed meat. It was not unusual for famous men to openly state, "I will not sue you for the law takes too long. I will ruin you." and then proceed to do so. In spite of all these immoral acts, a great nation was being built.

It wasn't until 1928 that the Federal Trade Commission went to court to force a company to cease using bribery in its sales program. The court upheld the defendant on the basis that the action was a common and acceptable trade practice. The National Association of Purchasing Agents volunteered to intervene on behalf of the FTC in the appeal, which resulted in the first federal court decision outlawing commercial bribery as an unfair trade practice. That was less than 50 years ago. An idea whose time had come. Is this ethic now to be extended overseas? Is this an idea whose time is now?

Let's examine the climate. I refer to three recent articles and quote from one by a U.S. banker speaking in Europe:

Certainly we must bow to local law and up to a point to the forces of local convention and custom, but we shouldn't compromise on matters of substance that could cause our company the support of the local constituency, the American people, their elected officials and regulators who are charged with enforcement of U.S. laws.

This statement raises many questions. It is similar to the practice of the U.S. extending its sovereignty overseas by prohibiting sales of goods from a Mexican subsidiary of a U.S. company to Cuba, only recently repudiated, and to the policy of interference in the affairs of foreign nations to promote democracy above other forms of government. I also question the implication that our elected officials are more moral than are we. Finally, is the support of the local constituency the end-all of moral judgments? Too often the local constituency admires the slick crook who got away.

The second article deals with an investment banker who spent six years as an investment adviser in Kuwait. He makes the point that an agent there performs a service and assumes a risk for which he is entitled to a payment, whatever it may be called. He says that the law prohibits any foreign company from doing business with the private sector unless it has a local agent and, if the company pulls out, the local agent is financially responsible for the default. In fact, the agent's identity is a matter of public record. To do business there any other way is both unethical and illegal.

Finally, there is a question of international competition. Business consistently insists that the rules be the same for all competitors. But the rules will not be the same if we outlaw payments to foreign agents. Our competitors will not follow suit. A recent article in the *London Daily Express* explains how bribes boost exports. Fees to foreigners are under Bank of England control, and a case is cited in which the amount exceeded the guidelines by three times because the contract was assured and was worth the large fee.

At a recent meeting at my company, thirty top executives had a heated discussion on a hypothetical case of extortion and bribery that I had sent out a few weeks before. The situation was described this way:

A U.S. corporation with only one business.

All raw material from one foreign source.

Competition supplied by other foreign sources.

A *ruinous* tax threatened in source country.

Tax would not be followed in other source countries (no OPEC).

High government official demands bribe to avoid tax.

Bribe to be deposited in Swiss bank account (clearly not for benefit of the people).

Payment of bribe against all moral and ethical principles of chief executive of the corporation.

What does the chief executive officer do? The alternatives are to:

Discuss with the board of directors.

Seek the aid of the State Department.

Report to the Securities and Exchange Commission.

Ask stockholders for approval to proceed to pay the bribe.

Publicize the situation in the source country.

Inform the United Church of Christ.

Write to the Better Business Bureau.

Make a public announcement that the company must be liquidated, at a cost of $100 million because it refuses to pay a $1 million bribe to a crooked politician.

Pay the bribe, save the company, hope for the best. Seek solace in semantics—that a bribe is sometimes a commission, in most circumstances for getting things to happen, sometimes to prevent them from happening.

The rules were that the situation could not be changed but alternatives could be added. I broke up the discussion after over an hour and called for a vote of "pay the bribe," "don't pay the bribe," or abstention. The outcome was 18 to 12 not to pay the bribe. There was an obvious age bias here, with the younger members favoring not to pay. Yet one of them said to me: "They may vote that way here, but if they were faced with a real live situation, they would pay because that means the most good for the most people." This may be unfair (perhaps unethical—are they the same?) but I wonder how many here would pay the bribe, not pay the bribe, or abstain? Take solace. Like all business school cases, there is no right answer.

Bribery payments do not raise the ire of stockholders, other businessmen, or adversely affect the multiple of the stock. At one recent annual meeting where bribery payments had been admitted, only one question was raised. And it was answered with, "I thought I was doing what was being done generally." Even when the corporations are supported overwhelmingly by government contracts, no legal action has resulted and the practice will be continued, according to some public announcements.

Much in the news today are tender offers, where one company seeks to acquire all or part of the stock of another. These tender offers are classified as friendly, which means the management and directors of the acquired company favor and recommend acceptance of the offer; or unfriendly, which means the opposite, that the offer should be rejected. The classifications imply that the first is moral, and the second immoral. In fact, there are companies which have a firm policy against making an unfriendly tender. Let's examine the ethical question.

Those in favor of restriction to only friendly tenders argue that it is application of the golden rule—"I do not want anyone to tender for my company's stock when I object, and therefore I should not tender for theirs if they object." It is kind of the old school-tie ethic—we in management must respect the "rights" of each other. We may compete in the marketplace, but not for the vote of the stockholders. Before leaving this side of the argument, some pragmatic reasons favor it—such as that an unfriendly management would be ineffectual and must be avoided.

The other side reasons that tenders, friendly or unfriendly, must be judged on ethical grounds in turn based on economic and legal reasons. Indeed, if all partners to the acquisition—stockholders and employees on both sides, customers, suppliers, government—benefit and there are no legal impediments, then all ethical questions are satisfied, even if management objects.

Corporate political contributions in the United States, with limited exceptions, are illegal. In spite of this, as with bribes, neither the stockholders nor the investment public let this affect their judgment of the companies. We recently checked a dozen security analysts on this question. Without exception, the gist of the replies was, "I wish my customers would react against such companies, but they don't. And I have to please my customers." Several great companies with excellent records stumbled in this regard and, although their employees may be irate and disgusted, the owners don't seem to be. Another friend who grew up in purchasing says, "There's no doubt that this is a serious problem. If students think they have to cheat to compete; if buyers think they have to deceive sellers because they themselves are being deceived; if workers think it's okay to steal because their bosses are stealing on a bigger scale—then the very foundations of our society are seriously threatened."

For the most part, the individuals involved in illegal political contributions have had scant punishment. The public generally has found this distasteful, which has helped again to lower the esteem in which it holds the business community. With few exceptions, other business leaders have not condemned the favoritism shown. Nor have auditors, alleged to have known of the illegal payments, been chastised. Lawsuits have been instigated by only a few dissident shareholders. And Congress has reacted by making the law more liberal, shortening the statute of limitations from five to three years, and cutting off investigations. This implies that Congress was fearful of finding its members in serious violation of the law, of which there is some considerable evidence.

Yet to extend this law to other countries makes no more sense than to extend the ethics of bribery (or commissions) to all situations. The United Church of Christ recently condemned the contribution of money to all foreign political campaigns. For this or other reasons, some major U.S. corporations with Canadian subsidiaries have recently announced that they will cease such contributions, even though the payments are completely legal in Canada and have been made for several years. Some of the Canadian press are irate; the implication is that the U.S. is more moral than its neighbors across the river. Who is to say whether the Canadian method of financing political campaigns is inferior to ours? Certainly the record does not say so.

Consumerism depends on both legal and ethical constraints. Yet there is abundant evidence that some legal constraints are not ethical. Bottles that cannot be opened by children are good. But what about the harm they do to the elderly, blind, or infirm who cannot open them either. How can we justify the inflation mandated by a rear window defroster or by a catalytic converter, later accused of causing even greater ills than those it eliminated. Is it wrong for a pharmaceutical company to ship a drug into a foreign country when it is positive of its efficacy even though the FDA has not released it in the United States?

Finally, isn't the environmentalist who insists on zero discharge completely immoral because he is dishonest, unless he is a hermit. Honesty is the first principle of morality. The only solution to pollution is dilution, and that does not allow for zero discharge.

Ethics plays a major role in how to treat, motivate, and supervise people. In order to correct past evils, discrimination must now favor minorities and women, creating a direct conflict with seniority, a time-honored ethic in American business and in fact legally binding. New laws make us favor the handicapped and the veteran. Yet we still discriminate in favor of those we like, a human although perhaps not an ethical practice. High moral principles prevent us from using industrial espionage but allow us to use the same people for tracking down suspected embezzlers. What about the other extreme: does an employee have the right, or even the obligation, to blow the whistle when he discovers illegal or or questionable moral acts by top management. Ethics will not allow taping of conversations without the knowledge of the parties, but is this binding in trying to uncover a criminal act?

The cost of ethics cannot be ignored. Job enrichment is ethical but often may not be economical. Cost versus benefit is the answer, but this involves intangibles difficult to quantify. Some people break laws because they think the laws are wrong. A recent *Business Week* article reported an astonishing number of price-fixing conspiracies, many justified in the minds of the offenders for this reason. Yet it seems to me that no actions to achieve market domination are wrong because concentration makes good economics.

One can argue that benefiting from a law when the law is wrong is immoral. We recently supplied a very large air pollution control device where the cost benefits to society were unfavorable. On the other side, we have dragged our feet on another device, expensive to us, where the cost benefits to society are probably favorable. I was surprised to learn recently that the companies who condemned passage of the Freedom of Information Act are the same companies who use it most frequently.

One of the most shocking violations of ethics in the press was the revelation that municipalities, specifically New York City, do all they can to camouflage the true facts of their financial situation in order to market their bonds. There is no SEC to police them and the public has been bilked. If industry took the same liberties, we would be in jail.

I believe the number of instances when a subordinate is asked to assist in or condone an immoral act are extremely rare. Yet I wonder how frequently management unwittingly creates a climate that tempts subordinates to cheat, not directly on their own behalf, but on behalf of the company and the company's measurement of performance. A suggestion that this condition exists is the recent case of cheating in the weight of grain exports. The direct beneficiary was apparently not the employee but the employer. This says to me that a company, to be prudent and moral, must be careful to avoid creating conflicts of interest for employees, lest the motivation backfire.

The single most dramatic event that called the public's attention to morals and ethics was, of course, the Watergate scandal. Could a Watergate happen in business? Could the actions of subordinates, motivated originally by good intentions, eventually become so distorted as to violate every moral principle? I fear the answer is yes. I see no constraints in one organization that do not exist in the other. Once basic morals are violated, their extension becomes much easier.

Morality varies with time and place. It is a moving target. There is danger in depending on what we did in the past in the United States to guide what we should do elsewhere in the future. But good ethics and high moral principles make for good companies because they give satisfactions to good people.

One last word. After all this, I have three conclusions:

There is no place for corporate codes of conduct; they end up as a bunch of cliches.

There is no place for college courses on business ethics; they end up without teaching anything.

If these two be true, it follows that there is no place for speeches on morals; you either have them or you don't. You decide.

5-2 Business Leadership and Moral Character*

W. Michael Blumenthal

When I first received the invitation to speak at this gathering, one of the things that caught my eye was the word "evening" in the name of your college. It occurred to me, after a hard day's work, that to study business administration in the evening was above and beyond the call of duty, and that the graduates of this venerable institution must be an unusually motivated group of people.

The news we hear and read and see these days is so uniformly bad that we feel an almost physical need for reasons to take pride in our country. I understand that the average age of this class is about 35 years and that its

---
*Speech at senior class banquet, University of Detroit, Evening College of Business Administration, May 3, 1975.

members have worked approximately seven years to attain their degrees. But this is only one of a number of ways in which the students of this class, and indeed of the entire college, depart from the stereotyped concept of the ordinary college student.

The dean informs me that the students of the evening college—all 1,040 of them—work full-time and attend classes part-time. It would be very difficult to think of a better example of energy, perseverance, and devotion to the ideal of self-betterment—not only on the part of the students themselves, but also of their wives or husbands. To those graduating today, then, I wish to express my own admiration and offer my sincerest congratulations.

Your academic achievements provide evidence that you have the mental equipment for continuing success in your professional careers—and this alone is a legitimate reason for congratulations, but the personal circumstances under which you have acquired your education are indicative of much more than "brain power."

You have shown that you have the ambition, the energy, the self-discipline, and the willingness to sacrifice some of your comforts today so that you, your family, your profession and your society can benefit from your increased competence and knowledge in the future. These are admirable qualities and are a strong assurance of success. But are they sufficient?

Are they sufficient for the moment when you may be called to cope with the problems which require a grasp of ends as well as means? Are they sufficient to lead a life in which you are at peace with yourself and with your conscience? I believe that everyone, and especially those aspiring to or already in, a position of leadership, needs something more. And that something more, I would suggest, is moral character.

The troubled and uncertain period through which we are passing, the dramatic and, in so many ways, tragic events of our recent past, the uncertainties which hang over our economic future, every aspect of our situation demands, I believe, that we renew our dedication to those traits of character that have too often been perceived as human weaknesses, rather than as virtues—honesty, justice, truthfulness, and compassion. There is nothing new, of course, in the idea of character, but I would argue that it has a peculiar relevance to the problems we face—as Americans and as business people—today.

Because you have chosen to prepare yourselves for careers in the business world, you should be aware that questions, extremely grave questions, are being raised about the moral standards or ethical behavior of the business world today. You all read the press and I don't think I need to draw diagrams to explain what I mean. As a result of Watergate and other recent incidents in our society, a certain number of our institutions have come under scrutiny, if not under attack, far more than ever before. And this kind of public concern has created a skeptical and sometimes hostile atmosphere in which the business community must do its work.

We cannot ignore this criticism or treat it as a passing phenomenon. There is nothing to suggest that it will just go away. The public opinion polls continue to show that the proportion of the public which takes a critical or hostile view of business is growing—and this has caused, and should cause, alarm within the business community.

The news media have turned the spotlight on many questionable activities. Let me cite a few examples. In just the past two weeks, we've seen reports on corporations which have broken the laws governing political campaign contributions; a large U.S. firm has been cited by the Securities and Exchange Commission for allegedly giving bribes to the president of a foreign country to gain a lower tax rate; another company has been accused of using a multimillion-dollar fund for payoffs to local officials of other nations to gain an unfair, and perhaps illegal, advantage over competitors. There have been similar reports of tax dodges, mishandling of pension funds, shoddiness of product quality, improper financial practices, discrimination in employment, and lack of concern for worker health and safety—all of which tend to raise questions of the ethical standards of the business enterprise, and to lower public confidence.

Faced with reports of this kind, the instinct of most businessmen is to rally to the defense of the business community. It is not true, they protest, that this conduct is par for the course. Indeed, if the misbehavior of a large corporation makes news, that is because the majority of large corporations do *not* misbehave. So it's unfair to tar all businesses with the same bad brush. It's unfair, because most businesses *do* adhere to ethical standards, *do* pay their taxes, *do* produce the best products they can, and so on and so forth.

All this is true enough, but I'm afraid it is not very helpful. I believe, in fact, that it misses the point. To leap to the defense of business in general whenever some specific abuse is uncovered only tends, in the public mind, to associate the one with the other. If businessmen are ethically strong and morally clean, why should they not be the first to denounce the abuses and malpractice which—far more than our critics in the media—threaten the survival of the free enterprise system?

A *Wall Street Journal* editorialist, who can hardly be suspected of being unfriendly to business, recently suggested that the business community reacts too little or not at all to the apparent questionable activities of some companies. The point he made is that more attention should be paid to the ethical aspects of business decisions. And with that premise, I agree.

I believe that the business community as a whole needs a more intimate and meaningful dialogue with its critics as well as its constituents. It seems to me that what we have today hardly deserves the name of dialogue at all. On one hand, we have the scandals, the charges, the countercharges, and suspicions which are so characteristic of the post-Watergate atmosphere. On the other, we find business spokesmen defending business as if it were a monolith, all of a piece; as if every suggestion of corporate wrongdoing, every proposal for change, were an attack on the free enterprise system as a whole. The result is nothing but confusion; we fail to come to grips. We are, as in those famous lines by Matthew Arnold: "... as on a darkling plain ... Where ignorant armies clash by night."

Let me suggest, then, that an entirely new approach is needed, a frankly moral approach, one which would begin with business taking a long, hard look at itself. This is not the sort of assignment, I am sorry to say, that the public will entrust to the National Association of Manufacturers, or to the Chamber of Commerce, or indeed to any of the groups traditionally associated with the defense of business, however earnest, honest, and competent they may be. We would all benefit, on the other hand, if the members of the business community, together with representatives of other segments of our society, would organize an institute or association to promote the idea of responsibility and ethics in business practices in the broadest sense.

Business executives, as I hardly need remind the graduates of this school, are professional people, just as lawyers and doctors and architects are professional people. But there is nothing in business life which corresponds to the bar associations, the AMA, or the American Society of Architects. Why then should business people not set up an association dedicated to defining and maintaining the standards of their profession? Such a group would deal with concrete questions of business ethics—not as an advocate defending business right or wrong, not from the view of a trade or industry association or on the basis of a concern for consumer relations, which the better business bureaus are already doing, nor, finally, in terms of a commitment to the economic and fiscal policies which are deemed to be in the interests of industry. Instead, it would focus on devising new ethical behavior codes to which all business would be expected to subscribe. These would correspond perhaps to the type of standards set up by professional associations. The founding members of this new group could be leaders from the business community, but it would draw as well on lawyers, the clergy, statesmen, philosophers, and others whose views would represent the moral concerns of society as a whole. This, indeed, would be the very point of the new departure which I am suggesting, that it would be, and would be seen to be, operating on behalf of society as a whole.

For business, the benefits of such an association would be twofold. First, by establishing the benchmarks of what is right and what is wrong, we are more likely to be able to fend off punitive, heavy-handed and possibly damaging legislation which the public itself will insist on if a degree of self-policing is not seen to be effective. And second, more importantly, I believe such action can provide a clear path for restoring confidence in business in our society—by improving the performance, and not merely the image, of our business organizations.

Ethical codes are no panacea, of course, even if they are enforced. But they do clarify our thinking and encourage socially useful behavior. With the public clamoring insistently for moral as well as social responsibility, I think the time is ripe for such action now. What I am suggesting, of course, is only one step, but an important one, toward restoring some confidence and trust in the relations between business and our society as a whole. Such a step, I feel, would do much to defuse many of the false issues which arise to plague us in the present unhealthy atmosphere.

The issue of bigness, for example. Indeed, a lot of the opprobrium cast on business seems to stem from an objection to bigness per se, from the feeling of personal helplessness which involvement with large institutions tends to create. It is a feeling, it seems to me, that goes deeper than intellectual argument, than the proposition that bigness makes for rigidity in the economy, for example, or the Jeffersonian tradition which asserts that freedom can flourish only in small communities. The fact remains that there is strength in size, and most of our people understand this, even when they rail against excessive concentration. Large institutions—in government, in business, in education—do give us efficiencies and economies of scale, which make higher living standards possible for greater numbers of people. The problem is how to make any organization, large or small, responsive and responsible to society and to the individuals it serves.

The debate about bigness, in any event, has been raging since the 19th century. It hardly helps to explain our present concerns. Perhaps there is no single, simple explanation. But one thing is certain: There is a moral tone in much of the criticism which has been levied against business in the past few years. The central issue is integrity, and much depends in the coming years on the forthrightness and courage with which we face up to that issue.

5-3 Public Trust in Business*

Frank T. Cary

Since you invited me to speak of the changes business must make to assure the future survival of our system, I'd like to talk about that today. I thought of many, but the one that tops the list is the need for business to put its house in order and regain the public trust. Without question, public trust in business is lower today than it has been for many years. In 1966, a national poll showed that 55 percent of Americans had confidence in business; today only 20 percent do. What has caused this decline? Many things, including business' own failure to communicate. But most of the decline is self-inflicted.

When some businesses turn out shoddy products, or engage in misleading advertising, or ignore customer complaints, the public gets sour on business as a whole. When some executives have to admit on a witness stand that they bribed

---
*Speech at the Junior Achievement, National Business Leadership Conference, Dallas, Texas, January 30, 1976.

foreign officials or illegally channeled corporate funds into political campaigns, the public believes this is standard business conduct. And when we read in the papers about corporate kickbacks and secret Swiss bank accounts, all business suffers.

Some businessmen have tried to excuse themselves by saying that everybody does it. Well, everybody doesn't do it, as you and I well know. However, given stories as entertaining as these, it is inevitable that some journalists and politicians will point to them as proof of a corporate crime wave. The time has come for those of us in business to put our house in order. Our challenge is to restore the faith of Americans in the basic competence and purpose of business. This requires a lot more than public relations efforts. We have to start by getting back to fundamentals—quality in the goods and services we provide, truth in advertising, being responsive to customer complaints. And we must have a code of conduct to govern our actions in the future.

I don't mean a single code for all companies. We have more than twelve million business enterprises in the United States. They represent every size and scope of operation. And given such diversity, a single code would lose its relevance and bite. What I am saying is this: each company should establish a code of conduct for itself—a code that everyone can understand. Having done that, I believe each company should make that code public: it should tell its employees, it should tell its stockholders, it should tell anyone else who wants to know what kind of conduct it will not tolerate, and what penalties will result. And from here on out, each company should hold its people to that code, beginning with its chief executive officer. He, more than anyone else, sets the moral tone of the company. He, more than anyone else, has the power to put a code in place. He, more than anyone else, has the power to see that the code is enforced. And if he does, it will work.

Some of you may have seen the report on codes of business conduct recently published by the *Business Roundtable.* The survey found many companies have excellent codes which they have lived by for years; and a great many companies are working toward this objective. I just hope many more will join them in the months ahead. Because the job begins with business itself and the attention it gives to standards of performance. Of all the changes we must make today to assure the survival of our system tomorrow, none has more urgency than rebuilding public confidence in business—a confidence that the young, in particular, can share.

A corporate office is a public trust. Restoring the good name of business deserves the best we can give it.

5-4 Corporate Reform: What's the Real Issue*

Irving S. Shapiro

The modern corporation gets high marks for its effectiveness as an instrument of production and distribution. Large corporations have been associated with rapid economic growth and important advances in technology. Big corporations have their uses, as even the staunchest critics concede.

Now these corporations face questions of a different kind, questions directed in particular at companies near the top on the "Fortune 500" list. They are not being asked if they are effective but if they are accountable, and if so, to whom? Is their power kept in control by the law, by their commercial competitors, by their stockholders, or, indeed, by anybody at all?

Some people have concluded very firmly that the big corporation has no legitimacy. An elaborate case has been constructed on that ground, and from it have come various prescriptions for reforming the corporation. The defense has not marshaled its arguments nearly as well, and with the conviction that time is slipping away I would like to offer, at least in a preliminary way, a case for the corporation.

We can concede that there are imperfections in corporations, but that does not mean we must accept as well-founded all of the criticism that is voiced. We can consider suggestions for change—I have a few offerings myself—but I still wish to challenge those who find endless fault with the corporate structure and want to perform major surgery on it. Much of the faultfinding is based on false information, and the more draconian prescriptions for corporate reform strike me as wrongheaded in the extreme. They would be counterproductive for the public and destructive to the economic system.

The complaints come down to three points:

First, it is alleged that big corporations are run by hired managers who are effectively beyond anybody's control. The boards of directors are either part of the power structure or are rubber stamps.

Second, it is believed that the outside forces that are supposed to keep corporations in check lack the power to do so, or have been coopted by the people they are supposed to regulate. Thus we are to dismiss—as just not doing the job—the combined force of the regulatory agencies, antitrust laws, market competition, unions, stockholders, and all the state laws governing corporate chartering.

The third general belief is that people in top management are narrow and often dishonest. They pay bribes, juggle the books, and slip corporate funds to politicians through Swiss "laundries." Though all corporate executives do not misbehave in this fashion, the story has it that consumers and employees still are victimized; scarce natural resources still are wasted; and the environment still is

*Speech at Commercial Club of Boston, April 20, 1976.

abused by pollution, because management is careless, insensitive, or just plain greedy.

Such beliefs have considerable public support. A recent survey done for the *Business Roundtable* reaffirms what other studies had shown before, namely, that people make a distinction between big business in particular, and the competitive enterprise system in general. The public is all for the enterprise system in principle, but a majority of the adult population (55 percent) believes that the big corporations got to be big by manipulating the market in some unfair way. A great many people—not a majority, but well over 40 percent—believe that the big corporations are above the law and can get away with just about anything. An even larger number—a clear majority—think big business ought to be regulated more tightly.

Sweeping Correctives Proposed

The message is that big business doesn't play by the rules, and something has to be done about it. Thus we see a variety of proposed correctives, many of them sweeping in nature, and no doubt more to come. Senator Philip Hart proposes to break up the big corporations. Senator Henry Jackson would bring the multinational oil companies more under the federal wing. Representative James Stanton would take the major firms in a number of "concentrated industries" and cut them into smaller pieces through changes in the antitrust laws. Former Supreme Court Justice Arthur Goldberg has revived an idea set forth years ago by Justice William Douglas, proposing that outside directors sit on corporate boards in a trustee capacity.

Professor George Lodge of Harvard and Professor Christopher Stone of the University of Southern California Law School have argued that the modern corporation should be more public and less private. To make that happen they and others suggest that boards should have a majority of outsiders; there should be a demographic representation of women and minorities; and labor should share the responsibility following West Germany's lead with codetermination.

Perhaps the most sweeping proposal is the one from Ralph Nader's Corporate Accountability Research Group. This calls for federal chartering of big companies with limits on the size, diversity, and share of market permitted to any one corporation.

The people pushing for federal chartering make no bones about their real objectives. They are not concerned merely with the official seal on a piece of paper—federal or state. That's a detail. What they really seek is control of the ground rules by which these firms operate. Advocates of federal chartering want to use the charter document to advance their own social and economic policies—policies which by and large they have not been able to sell in the public forum of ideas. Their prescription would turn over the controls almost completely to Washington, where the perception of the proper goals for business is based on the pressure-group techniques that beset our national capital.

Chartering is a phony issue. The real issue is power. Much of the power over business already resides in such agencies as the SEC, the EPA, and the Justice Department. With federal chartering we would see the creation of a super SEC, not only displacing the states but probably also scooping up much of the authority of other federal regulatory bodies—in short, more centralization, less freedom all around.

Adequate Control Already Exists

What is the counter argument? As I see it, the prescriptions for major change are deeply flawed in their premises. What is taken as a "given" is largely a myth. There is no runaway corporate power in the U.S. The existing body of law and regulation provides broad-ranging control of corporations, and the fact that some of these corporations are quite large in no way exempts them from that control.

Du Pont is as good an example as any. There is no point in boring you with a full list of the agencies monitoring our activities. It is much the same alphabet that applies to other big corporations—EPA, OSHA, FDA, FTC, SEC, ICC, FPC, and so on. As for the overall scale of the involvement, suffice it to say we have the equivalent of 180 employees working full time just to keep the federal, state, and local governments informed through the reports Du Pont must file.

Like other businessmen, I have a very hard time understanding the charge that somehow all these governmental activities miss their mark. We in Du Pont find government regulation to be persistent, effective, and almost ubiquitous.

As for competition in the marketplace, it is vigorous and effective, and no respecter of corporate size or concentration. The price and quality of a firm's products and services are not related to its share of the market. There is no reason to believe, for example, that steel would be cheaper if there were twice as many steel companies; or that gasoline would become cheaper if the integrated oil companies were chopped into separate units for production, refining, and distribution; or that consumers would be better off if the Big Four in the auto industry were to become the Big Eight or the Big 16. Economic theory as well as the history of that industry suggest the opposite. The relative price of automobiles has come down as the size of the manufacturers has gone up. It takes fewer hours of work for a typical person to earn enough money to buy a car now than it did in 1950 or 1920.

The impact of market forces is only too real and often quite painful. Du Pont was recently reminded of that. Our company is a large producer of man-made fibers, and these are made primarily out of oil and natural gas. When the price of those raw materials went soaring in 1974 and 1975, other market factors made it impossible for Du Pont to raise the selling price of fibers enough to cover increased costs. As a result, earnings declined very sharply.

The point to stress is that the marketplace dictated this result despite all the theoretical arguments about size and concentration. Critics find easy generalizations to dismiss competition as ineffectual for big companies, but in fact it is an everyday reality and a stern taskmaster.

The net effect of federal chartering would be to turn corporations into what a Harvard professor calls "nationally chartered community-oriented collectives." That would be a fundamental break with America's past. With an eye to common sense and to the national self-interest, it would seem logical to make such a move only if the economic system we have is failing badly and is so deeply flawed as to be beyond repair. This dismal condition does not exist, and it is therefore hard to find merit in proposals that would point the nation toward more federal control of economic activity.

Deterrent to Investment

On a more down-to-earth basis, one may also raise questions as to how many investors would continue to risk their capital in these "community-oriented collectives," and how venturesome and farsighted the management would be when confronted with the problems of constituency politics.

Large corporations must make commitments years in advance. To build a new plant or open up a new product line, they must work on lead times of two to 10 years or more. The $1 billion Du Pont will spend for construction in the next year or so will not begin to pay out for more than five years. Managers and directors will put that kind of money on the line only if they have reasonable confidence in their forecasts, and if they feel they have reasonable control over the decisions that will make for profit or loss.

Suppose Du Pont's board were constructed to achieve what some people call "corporate democracy," with directors appointed to represent women, blacks, environmentalists, labor, and various public interest or community groups. I question whether the individual directors would in fact represent those constituencies, but even if they did, could they run a chemical business? Could such a board recognize a successful management strategy reaching five to 10 years into the future? Would it back such a strategy to the tune of hundreds of millions of dollars a year? Or would it be whipsawed by competing interest groups and be unable to set any enduring policies at all?

Much of the criticism of the American political system goes to the point that government is too short term and fragmented in its approach. Yet the prescriptions for corporate reform could easily result in a system that would have to operate much like the Congress, with constant mediation, compromise, and logrolling. It is ironic that some of the people most unhappy about the legislative process are the same people who want to push business organizations in the same direction.

Business organizations could be more farsighted—there is room for improvement on this score—but I seriously doubt that the more extreme proposals for reform would produce such improvement.

A better case can be made for leaving the basic structure as it is, and letting constituent democracy exercise its voice in the marketplace. Where there are overriding national concerns—as for example, with the need for conservation of energy resources or for pollution control—there are other, more appropriate mechanisms of control. We do not need to remodel and in effect politicize the economic system to put into effect a national energy or environmental policy. Such jobs should be done by government in Washington, not by trying to put a miniature governmental structure into the boardrooms of the 500 largest corporations.

The groups that make up the American society have a right to their views about corporate performance. They have a right to criticize when they have facts showing that corporations are doing wrong and to seek governmental action when that is needed. None of that, though, constitutes a right to a seat on the board.

This may sound like a defense of the status quo: Bring the wagons into a circle. Fight change!

That is not my point. I think business must do a better job of keeping its house in order and in convincing people that this is being done. That applies at all levels including the board of directors.

Business leaders ought to be taking a hard look at the functions of a corporate board, what it takes to discharge those functions properly, and what the board ought to be showing the outside world about itself. There may be room for improvement all around.

I see five basic jobs for a board of directors:

1. To select the company officers and provide for the succession of people in the key spots.
2. To determine the broad policies and establish the general direction of effort of the enterprise.
3. To set the performance standards—ethical as well as commercial—against which the management is to be judged.
4. To monitor management's performance in meeting overall strategy and operational goals.
5. Last—and this is more controversial—it is the job of the board to keep people informed about its policies and standards, and about steps being taken to keep the organization responsive to the needs of the people whose lives it affects in a significant way.

If you agree that this list of duties is reasonable, we ought to work toward a number of conditions.

Corporate boards should be composed of people of the highest competence and integrity. There is simply no substitute for quality. Directors should be sought to provide the organization with perspective both about detailed aspects of the business and about the societal factors that ought to be considered in any organization that affects the lives of thousands of people. The first question that ought to be asked about any candidate for a directorship is, "Will he or she help provide informed and principled oversight of the corporation's management and policies?"

Corporations need more windows to the outside world. Where they do not have a good selection of outside directors, they should get them. It is important to have insiders who know the business, but outsiders can bring added strengths and different perceptions to the boardroom.

Directors Should be Carefully Chosen

What is most important in setting the mix is to end up with people looking over management's shoulder who are inquisitive, independent, and equipped to make decisions that may not be easy or popular. Directors must be carefully chosen: Windows are not the same as window dressing.

It is sometimes argued that proper oversight is best assured by a majority of outsiders on a board, but in some respects I classify this, along with federal chartering, as a phony issue. The involvement of outsiders—in more than token numbers—can contribute to the open and inquisitive atmosphere which contributes so much to responsible board operations. What is crucial, though, is the climate in which decisions are made, not the ratio of insiders to outsiders. Above all, I believe that quotas should be avoided at all costs. Quotas have nothing to do with quality.

Boards should be working organizations in every sense of the word. In this day and age there should be no spot at the table for those willing only to show up once a month for a two-hour meeting. Some of the trouble big companies have gotten into can pretty clearly be traced to inattention on the part of the directors. Where that situation exists, companies should weed out the deadwood.

For a board member to do his job properly he or she has to have access to relevant data and staff help. The idea of equipping directors with private staffs does not seem practical or productive. That almost guarantees an adversarial climate in an area where nothing is gained through adversarial proceedings. It is not as though we needed teams of lawyers to litigate board matters. Presumably all the people working on behalf of a corporation are on the same side. Directors ought to be able to obtain the information they need by calling upon company specialists in production, marketing, and research, and those close to the legal, financial, employee relations, and public affairs problems as well.

There are a lot of prescriptions for organizing the work of a board. Students of such matters have come up with suggestions for committees on audit, finance, and other areas, with outside directors having control of certain committees. Structure is important. Among other things, it's a signal to the outside world of how the store is being run. Once again, though, formulas can lead us astray. The first concern should not be with appearances but with the best way for a board to ensure adequate checks and balances, given the people it has. A strong chairman of the audit committee is vital, but if the strongest candidate for that assignment happens to be an insider, so be it.

Free Discussion Needed

Whatever the organizational structure, there should be a climate encouraging free discussion. There should be written reports for directors to study before meetings. Management should be available for private discussion. There should be freedom to dissent with no disagreeable reactions and no "ganging up" on directors who are out of step with the majority.

Boards should prepare a written statement setting forth the kinds of corporate conduct which will and will not be tolerated. Given the recent examples of corporate wrongdoing and the public feeling that these may be commonplace, the leaders of corporations have no choice but to state some convictions for the record.

Codes of conduct have been discussed at great length, and the consensus seems to be that a universal code that would fit all businesses cannot be drafted except perhaps in broad generalities that would sound good but mean little. Instead, the current view seems to be that each company should draft its own code. I have no quarrel with this conclusion provided that a basic ground rule is observed: Make it clear and make it public.

In thinking about this I am helped by working from an analogy with the Sherman Act. It makes a distinction between per se offenses and actions which are right or wrong in specific circumstances. A similar distinction can be made in drafting a corporate code. Every one ought to include prohibitions of certain kinds of conduct which cannot be justified regardless of circumstances. Thus, for example, secret bribery of government officials, whether at home or abroad, subverts the governmental process. Similarly, one could not justify shipping to another nation a product that is inherently unsafe regardless of whether that nation has had the wit to preclude such a product.

On the other hand, the question of corporate political contributions in nations which do not prohibit such contributions is a matter for each company to decide for itself. Certainly our national mores in this respect are not the necessary standard for conduct in nations which have found no meaningful distinction between individual and corporate political funding.

Where there is some difficulty in deciding how the ethical standards ought to be applied, I go along with a practical test: Would you be comfortable with public disclosure of the standards and the reasoning behind them?

Let me take this a step further and make one final point regarding disclosure. Most of us in the business world keep things too close to the vest. It has been said many times that corporate management ought to be more open and candid with the public, and I believe that can be applied just as well to boards of directors. There is a communications problem.

Many critics of corporate boards are people who have not themselves had any experience on such boards. The way they think a board works, and the way it actually works, may well be entirely different. This ought to concern us, because public opinion and government policy may crystallize around these perceptions of corporate behavior, however incorrect the perceptions may be.

Let me read you a comment by another professor. There is a lot of truth in what he says.

What is most evidently missing today and needs to be restored is a measure of mutual trust and respect. As things stand, we are settling into a cycle in which the laws wielded against corporations are products of little more than mutual frustration, a cycle which is giving the businessman fits, and the public little to show for it.

When the evidence points to an acute problem like work-related cancer, society, distrustful of what is going on within the corporation's walls, and kept at arm's length from the loci of corporate decision making, sees little choice but to slap together a battery of new regulations even before it is adequately informed. There are obvious costs to both sides.

I agree. If trust and respect are lacking it is not just because of recent, well-publicized misbehavior by some companies; it is also because for years we in business have not taken the public enough into our confidence. We have not let people see enough of what we do and what we stand for. All too often the corporate chief executive officer has been a cardboard figure and the company's policies as they relate to the public interest have been unknown, or so wrapped in "P.R." as to lack credibility.

Those of us in business can do better by ourselves than that. We ought to have the wit and ingenuity to come up with some communications ideas that would give the public a more meaningful picture and more information about the real policies and practices of our businesses.

Going Public is Not Painful

Some companies have begun to move in this direction. The Bank of America, which is now putting together a corporate disclosure policy, is a case in point. In Du Pont, we have established a public register relating to political contributions by members of management. Some chief executives have taken to the hustings to tell their story, much like a political officeholder, and they are having an impact, at least insofar as their own companies are concerned. There undoubtedly are many other techniques for going public. The important point, I think, is that more openness is a necessary development and we should welcome it. Going public is not painful and it helps dispel the aura of suspicion.

Big corporations have made extraordinary contributions to society. They have many more to make in the future. Most people accept that. What they question now is whether the system keeps these big companies accountable, and whether the people in charge have the integrity and intelligence to do their job properly.

The burden of proof now falls on us in business, and the jury we must convince is some 220 million Americans, not self-appointed pressure groups and not a small number of theoreticians, however erudite they may be, who wish to restructure the economic system to suit biases the public does not share.

I have no doubt that the burden can be carried successfully if the public can get to know the men managing our major companies and if those men will tell it like it really is.

6 The Present Economic System and the Moral Dilemma

6-1 Ethical Confusion and the Business Community*

Albert W. Levi

Ethical problems in any walk of life are hardly new, and certainly they are not new in business. But public scandals and private revelations cause a great focusing of light on dark places. They stir up the placid waters. They cause consternation among the culprits, injured amazement among the unsophisticated, moral indignation in the public at large. Like any enormous and powerful searchlight too, they generate almost as much heat as they do light.

The recent incidents which have rocked the business and industrial community are no exceptions. The cases of possible abuses in connection with stockpiling scarce materials, the Billie Sol Estes incident, and the conviction of high executives in the electrical industry have elicited varied responses. Without any effort to be scientific or systematic, I have spoken (where opportunity permitted) to businessmen about these events in the newspaper headlines. And on the basis of my private poll, I can state with confidence that with respect to ethics, great confusion reigns within the business community. Let me report below just a small sample of the varied and characteristic comments which have been made to me.

A. Ethics is ethics and business is business. Profits are one thing and moral squeamishness is another. You have to make a choice.
B. I'm a businessman and I try to be ethical, but when others in my field cut corners morally, I don't see how I can stay in business if I don't follow suit.
C. Morality is terribly vague, it seems to me. The churches say one thing, the bosses of my company another, and I guess the government even something different. Who's right?
D. Business as a whole *is* ethical. Of course you'll always find a few cheaters and crooks, but they're built that way. They'd cheat whatever they worked at.
E. If a man follows the Gospel he can't go wrong. Too many business executives have let the basic religious truths out of their sight. That's our trouble.

---
*From Joseph W. Towle, ed., *Ethics and Standards in American Business* (Boston: Houghton Mifflin Co., 1964), Chapter 2, with updating by the author. Reprinted with permission.

Each of these statements, for all its colloquialism of expression, states or presupposes an attitude with respect to business ethics. *A* says: Ethics and business are by nature incompatible. *B* says: In competitive activity the morally lowest necessarily sets the standard. *C* says: Morality is a matter of "knowledge," and with plural answers, there is no way to choose between them. *D* says: Immorality is a defect of personal character. It will always exist. *E* says: Morality means following the rule of religion.

It is obvious that some of these statements are highly debatable if not definitely false. It is also obvious that several of them are incompatible with one another and that, since they are held by reputable members of the business community, they indicate the doubts and uncertainties, the confusions and inconsistencies which pervade the thinking of that community in the matter of its relation to standards of moral behavior.

In the brief space at my disposal, I cannot pretend to resolve this mare's nest of confusion and so set the business community clearly and unhesitatingly upon its moral way. I want, however, to do three things. First, I want to distinguish three senses of "ethics" that are relevant to the problems of business ethics and to indicate why I believe that two of them offer unrewarding paths, while in the third conception lies our best hope of real reform. Second, I want to develop that third concept in such a way as to illuminate the permanent and underlying dilemma of the business community and to suggest what I believe is the only way out. And, finally, I want to fit this suggestion into the general framework of what has been happening within the development of Western industrial society for the last five hundred years.

II

No questions like "What is right?" or "Why should I be moral?" (the one asking for moral content, the other for the source of moral obligation) can be asked in a vacuum. They are meaningful only if given a context of group membership and societal demand. My roles determine my obligations. General questions like "What is right?" are therefore convertible into a whole series of more specific inquiries: "What is expected of me as a father? as a resident of Missouri? as a friend?" But for the problem of business ethics, the relevant questions are, I think, three: What is expected of me as a member of my religious group?; What is expected of me as a citizen of the United States? What is expected of me as a member of the business community? The answer to the first question yields the *religious* criterion of morality, the second the *legal* criterion of morality, the third the *professional* criterion of morality. It is my belief that part of the ethical confusion of the business community lies in not really knowing which of these questions to ask, and that the road out lies in recognizing that the first two, valuable as they are to a limited extent, are not the crucial questions. The crucial question is the third.

Naturally, a businessman is also a citizen of the United States. It is therefore a first approximation of his duty that he act within the requirements of the law. This is necessary, but it is not sufficient. It is minimal, not optimal. And the reason is clear. The common conscience of our time is not entirely approving of those who keep just one step within the law. To equate "legality" and "morality" does not satisfy our sense of the true claims of ethical behavior. For law imposes sanctions "from outside." These sanctions enforce not what a man chooses for himself, but what impersonal legislative enactments and judicial decisions demand of him. With this he loses his moral autonomy. In being guided only by "the lawful," motivation for moral behavior becomes simply prudential. The motive for "moral" behavior becomes an attempt to escape punishment or reprisal. "I will do," says the businessman or industrialist, "anything for which the law cannot punish me." The guide to conduct becomes a negative fear, not a positive conception of his duty. *Legality* is, therefore, not enough.

But if ethics as "action within the law" is not enough, ethics as behavior within the requirements of religious demand is too much. The first is too modest in what it requires, the second too utopian. I pass over the extreme ambiguity of religious precepts as applied to the businessman's life, and to the fact that religious sects are multiple and that many people either have no religion or take lightly what religion they do have. The fact remains that in a secular and a pluralistic society, even the tenets of the Judeo-Christian tradition cannot be taken as definitive for the business and industrial life. We can all sympathize, I think, with the attempts of ministers, priests, and rabbis to raise the moral level of their congregations through sermons, exhortations, prayers, and personal example, and if from time to time they succeed in this attempt, we can only marvel and wish them well. But in American society in the twentieth century, it would be folly to believe as *E* did in the quotation above that "If a man follows the Gospel, he can't go wrong." A guide to conduct originated in the Middle East over two thousand years ago could hardly be *directly* relevant to the enormously complicated cases of technologized industry. Even the effort required to make "the spirit" of religious truths applicable to the modern world is beyond the individual man and the various churches, none of which speak in a voice recognized by the whole of the business community. *Religion*, therefore, is also not enough.

It is the third question which is crucial: "What is expected of me as a member of the business community?" The answer to this question can hardly be provided by any agency but the business community itself. But this, in turn, presupposes that there *is* such an entity as "the business community" and that it speaks with clear and authoritative voice. Here is where the real problems lie, and I shall turn to a brief consideration of them in the next section. But they all hinge on one question: "What does it mean for business to be a profession?" For I think that we have now discovered which of the senses of "ethics" is most relevant to the problems of the business community. Ethics as action within the law is not enough. Ethics as behavior within the requirements of religious demand is too vague and inaccessible. What we seek is the concept of *ethics as responsible professional behavior*. And we might have discovered this all along if we had simply looked at the motto written over the portals of the Harvard Business School—TO MAKE BUSINESS A PROFESSION.

III

When *A* in the quotation above said, "Ethics is ethics and business is business; profits are one thing and moral squeamishness another; you have to make a choice," he was speaking for a large segment of his fellow men. And it does serve to call attention to the diametrically opposed point of view of a "business" and a "profession" as ordinarily understood. The distinction between them is simple, and it is a logical distinction. The aim of business is *profit*. The aim of a profession is *the performance of a service*. It is a matter of emphasis first of all. The true businessman keeps his eye *on the reward*. The true professional man keeps his eye *on the activity*. If a doctor thinks more of the fee than of the patient, he is a businessman even if he spent six years in the best medical school in America. If the owner of a bakery takes pride in his bread, tries to make the best bread in his city, turns out a loaf that graces his own table, and is less interested in the volume of his yearly profit than in the quality and reputation of his merchandise, he is a professional man (a craftsman) even if he has never graduated from college.

Naturally, from this distinction certain secondary consequences follow. The man who is interested chiefly in profit shifts his activity in accordance with the promise of profits. If he is a capitalist, he may sell all his holdings in cereals one day to invest them in aircraft production the next. If he is an executive, he may move from personnel manager of a large department store to second vice-president of a utilities company without any feeling of permanent loyalty to either. If he is a small entrepreneur, he may sell his grocery store to go into the real-estate business. In a profession, this is almost impossible. It is almost unthinkable that a college professor in the humanities should after ten years turn to engineering because the salaries are better there, or that a physician after practicing medicine for half a lifetime should change to corporation law because of increased financial rewards. Men whose eyes are on the activity rather than the profit are more *anchored* in their way of life. They are more committed to their professional occupation. They are, therefore, in general more *responsible* in the performance of their work. *Commitment* and *responsibility* are thus a mark of the professions rather than the businesses, and if business is to be made a profession, it needs to devise methods whereby *emphasis upon the activity, commitment*, and *responsibility* become the common property of members of the business community.

I am well aware that this too sounds "utopian," that my distinction between the "business" concentration upon profit and the "profession" putting the activity first and the profit second squares badly with the practice of some of our fee-hungry doctors, lawyers, and engineers, even ministers of the Gospel. But this does not impair the *logic* of the position. It only indicates the falling off which results when the business mentality at its worst—all pervasive and dangerous—corrupts the very strongholds of professionalism itself. The distinction between profit and service, reward and activity, is a matter of emphasis—obviously not of complete separation—but the relation between them in the distinction is subtle. The physician who takes money *for* healing is, as I have said, a businessman; the physician who needs money *in order that* he can heal is a professional man. The teacher who considers his salary *as a reward for* his work is a businessman; the teacher who realizes that his salary is *what permits him to* exercise his passion for bringing knowledge where before there was only ignorance is a true professional.

Let me pass now from the "logic" of the situation to its more customary aspects although even here we shall find that the two are not unrelated. There are, I think, even in the popular mind three unfailing characteristics of a profession: (1) education beyond the usual level, (2) the primary duty of service to the public, and (3) the right to responsible self-government. They are interrelated aspects.

A profession demands a traditional training—time spent in a professional school which inculcates standards of performance and responsibility. But the pursuit of (1) is not the aim of professional life, it only leads to (3). True professions consider themselves not merely as individuals but as social entities; as a persisting guild or professional association, they establish continuity and order. Such guilds or professional associations, where they have shown themselves worthy, have been entrusted by society itself with the right (a) to perpetuate professional standards and (b) to enforce these standards by penalizing their infractions. Not, I think, until the business community has been *professionalized*, until that is, it too requires education beyond the usual level, recognizes its primary duty as that of service to the public, forms its own body to formulate business standards, and *itself* penalizes their infractions, will it be granted by a skeptical public the right of self-government, relieved of the threat of hostile (government or public) interference. The possibility of business becoming "ethical" is bound up with the possibility of its professionalization.

We can now see more clearly why the choice of the meaning of "ethics" which I espoused for business in Section II of this article involved a "professional" rather than a "legal" or a "religious" criterion of morality. For, in the last analysis, the question for consideration is, "Where should the responsibility for the enforcement of morality originate?" Shall it be the individual, the society, the professional body? In the case of business, my own preference (and I think that of the enlightened businessman likewise) would be the professional body. The grounding of business ethics in religion or personal morality leaves the individual as ultimate enforcer, and while I think we must leave as much of this to the individual sense of responsibility as possible, I am not optimistic about its success. Nor do I think (unless in the case of last resort) business morality should be presided over by courts and administrative (legal) agencies. I prefer the guild or professional association as the delegated representative of society to control the standards and ethically limit the activities of the business community. But it should have to be a guild or professional association much more stringent and responsible than the American Medical Association, the National Association of Manufacturers, the American Bar Association, or the Chamber of Commerce. For it must not be a mere lobbying association for economic advantage, but a board of review of obligations and standards. And this will involve a complete psychological re-orientation of the business mentality so that its central concern is no longer "my racket and its loot" but "my service function and its duties." But this brings us further than merely to the solution of the ethical confusions of the business community. It brings us squarely up against certain changes which have characterized the development of Western industrial society for the last five hundred years.

IV

The ethical behavior of any segment within society is generally not without roots in the more general goals and aspirations of that society as a whole. And in the case of the business community, which makes up by far the most numerous occupational group, it can almost be said that its moral level reflects with perfect accuracy the moral level of the wider society of which it is a part. If then one asks for "a complete psychological re-orientation of the business mentality," this is almost tantamount to asking for a re-orientation in the thinking of the total society itself.

Professionalism is one of the most valuable elements in the social structure. In a world where the nineteenth-century reliance upon the self-determining code of the autonomous individual has broken down, the group becomes increasingly important, and group demands for the meeting of professional obligations, responsibility in human relations, and excellence in performance have a cogency and a persuasiveness which neither personal bewilderment nor impersonal outside power can match. But it would be folly not to recognize that the very essence of professionalism—emphasis upon the activity rather than the reward, upon the performance of a service rather than profit—goes against the very grain of the mentality of Western civilization since the breakdown of the medieval social order almost five hundred years ago.

Modern capitalism is based upon a philosophy of individualism which, when spelled out, implies that the basis of society is to be found not in responsibilities but in *rights*. The individual enters the world with a "natural right" to freely control his property and to follow his economic self-interest independent of obligation to society or duty to serve it in any way. The possession of property and the direction of industry are thought to require no special justification because they are based on rights which men possess quite apart from any obligation to contribute to general happiness or an over-arching social purpose.

Lest one believe that it has never been otherwise, it is important to remember that medieval economic structure enthroned principles which were just the reverse. Property and economic activity existed to promote the ends of society (or of God); society did not exist to promote the aims of business enterprise. Each individual found his place in the economic order (whether as farmer, craftsman, or merchant) according to the service he performed, and remuneration was not independent of *social function* but a consequence of its claim. Since the fourteenth century, it has slowly become otherwise. The breakdown of church authority, the rise of the urban middle classes, industrialization, a philosophy of individual rights has gradually undermined the organic functionalism of medieval society.

What has happened, then, over the past five hundred years has been the gradual development of a "functional" into an "acquisitive" society, a society where the chief subject of economic emphasis is the performance of social role into a society whose whole tendency and preoccupation is the enthronement of money and the acquisition of wealth. It is within this setting that the contemporary problem of "business ethics" must be seen—the conflict between the professional demand for responsible service and the exclusively business demand for profits. Within this setting, unfortunately, it is by no means certain that "a complete psychological reorientation of the business mentality" is possible. If not, the hope of committing business to the canons of responsible professional behavior is only a dream, a moralist's vision without consequence in reality.

I am sorry to end on so somber a note, but it is unavoidable. The specific ethical confusion of the modern business community is grounded in the larger issue of the destiny of Western economic society. Problems which began with the consequences of specific public business scandals can only lead to considerations which require the formulation of a complete economic and social philosophy.

1977 Update by Professor Levi

As the references in the second paragraph indicate, this paper was written between fifteen and twenty years ago (and originally published in Joseph W. Towle, *Ethics and Standards in American Business*, now out of print). There is little I would change today. The argument stands. The crisis is if anything even more acute. And it now has the uncomfortable flavor of *déjà vu*. For our most recent scandals only present the spectacle of business corruption on a more massive scale. The alleged illegal political contributions of Gulf Oil, Braniff, and American Airlines to the Nixon re-election campaign, the resignation of 3 M's top management for a similar offense, the steamy issue of payoffs for expresident Nixon's increase of federal milk price supports on behalf of American Milk Producers Inc., the charges of ITT's intervention in the internal political affairs of Chile, the suicide of Eli Black of United Brands in the wake of underwriting international bribery in Honduras and Italy, as well as the admitted bribes of Lockheed in Japan and the Netherlands, Gulf Oil in South Korea, Exxon in Italy, and of Northrop, Grumman Aerospace, Ashland Oil, Merck and Co. and others elsewhere, show that economic immorality has become not simply a glaring exception but a corporate way of life. The ancient transgressions of Billie Sol Estes and the electrical industry have proliferated into a tolerated climate of business behavior. This presents the issue squarely. Under these circumstances has corporate capitalism a viable future?

The seventeenth century was the high-water mark of the divine right of kings. But a hundred years later it was gone with the wind. The free enterprise system does not exist by divine right. And its time, I think, is running out. The socialist alternative becomes stronger and more persuasive to the idealistic young each day. And socialism as an economic philosophy has been spreading more broadly over the underdeveloped world since the Marxist revolutions.

Many who once believed that "one must always expect a few rotten apples in the barrel" are slowly becoming persuaded that the entire capitalist system is a barrel of rotten apples. Especially within the capitalist countries themselves cynicism is growing and the common man becomes increasingly impatient of corporate transgression.

One thing has become eminently clear. The future of the corporate system hinges upon its capacity for self-reformation. Things cannot continue as they are. And a capitalism incapable of self-policing in the direction of acceptable standards of moral behavior is doomed to a righteous extinction.

6-2 Towards New Corporate Goals:
Co-existence with Society*

Donald E. Schwartz

The debate over the social responsibilities of corporations obviously is not a new one. Forty-six years ago, Professors Dodd and Berle explored the question of whether corporation management owed a duty to shareholders or to the larger

---

*From *Georgetown Law Journal*, October 1971, Vol. 60, pp. 57-109, with updating and revisions by the author. Copyright © 1971 by the *Georgetown Law Journal*. Reprinted with permission.

public.[1] Whether corporations have the power to make gifts of the corporation's money to charities is certainly not a new question,[2] and corporate managers have long professed that they owed an obligation to the general public served by the corporation.[3]

Important changes, however, are noticeable in the more recent challenges to corporations and their managers. One obvious change is that there are new participants in the debate. The question of corporate responsibility and managerial duties is no longer exclusively, nor even primarily, a concern for academicians. It is, rather, a populist issue which has produced comments from politicians, the general press, and young concerned citizens.[4] At its basis, the new attention being accorded corporate social responsibility is prompted by manifold problems of our society, including concern over the environment, product safety, discrimination, and foreign policy, all of which are seen as having a relationship to corporate pursuits. Since these problems appear to be increasing in size and impact, efforts to deal with them are being pushed more aggressively.

The Structure of Financial Institutions

Financial institutions have become the most important stockholders of large corporations. External pressures applied to institutions to support socially responsible activities by corporations conflict heavily with their internal pressures, the most obvious of which is the imperative to invest for maximum profit. Thus, the Austin Report urges Harvard University to continue to invest on the basis of profit alone.[5] While no institution has indicated a departure from this policy—all seem to regard the purchase of securities as a socially neutral act—the response of some institutions has been to organize a separate independent mutual fund whose policy would be to select investments utilizing criteria of social performance as well as the more conventional profit performance. Presumably, disclosure of this policy would restrict investors to those who share that goal, without imposing it on others who have only a profit expectancy from their investments.[6]

But behavior as a shareholder differs from behavior as an initial investor. Again, there are pressures which result in institutions favoring the policies of management with whom the institution often enjoys profitable business relations.[7] As a shareholder, however, one cannot escape having to make a choice on specific public policy questions. Neutrality disappears as shareholder proposals compel either support or opposition to management. When managers confront difficult choices, are those choices to be dictated entirely by profit analysis? If those choices result in support for activities which the institution believes are against public policy, does the institution and its constituency become a participant in conduct they abhor?

It is a simple task to state the legal rule governing the investment conduct of institutions. Their managers are fiduciaries, required to act in the best interests of their beneficiaries.[8] This simple legal proposition, however, is not helpful. The real question arises in attempting to define what is "in the best interest of the beneficiaries." For that question there is no simple answer. Almost any public interest proposal can be described as beneficial in the long run, if for no other reason than the fact that voluntary action will forestall or prevent legislation dealing with the objectionable conduct. Because there may be some truth to this argument, it is almost impossible to conclude that a vote by a fiduciary in favor of a public policy question would be against the best interests of the beneficiaries. Consequently, the fiduciary acts almost entirely without the benefit of any legal standard.

It is at this point that the fiduciary's real problems may begin. If he decides that the best public policy should dictate the manner of his vote, he then faces the difficult task of determining where corporate management has failed in its public duties.[9] On what information will he act? What cost will he incur in determining the fact?

Thus, one is brought to a final question in this inquiry into institutional response: Since institutions usually represent the accumulated savings of many investors or represent various constituencies, who is to decide for the institution? This question is especially important where largely subjective values are to be applied in deciding upon socially desirable conduct. Where such a value judgment is required, the most important issue may concern the question of whose judgments are counted. The problem of who decides has a wide effect. It pertains to pensioners and beneficiaries of trust funds where portfolios are professionally managed, to mutual fund shareholders, to universities whose constituencies are varied and whose lines of authority are blurred, and to insurance policy holders.

Testing the Institutions

Although brokers, as members of the financial community, are part of the monolithic structure essentially committed to management, they are not financial institutions. Institutions usually act through professional managers who have the legal right to exercise voting power without prior consultation with those holding the beneficial or underlying interests.

The largest institutional holders are the private pension plans, wherein the exclusive right to vote is conferred upon a trustee, generally a bank, by a trust instrument. Where this right exists, the trustee rarely consults the beneficiary about how the shares should be voted, but usually votes with management.[10] It should be borne in mind that some pension plans represent sizable constituencies, such as union members, yet there is no evidence that the membership of those organizations has been consulted on the voting of the trust shares. Only within the most quasi-political institution, the university, does there seem to be any serious question as to the appropriateness of how the shares shall be voted by the nominal authority.[11]

Corporation Law and Social Responsibility

Lawyers have always been in the vanguard of any discussion about the role of corporations and other issues dealing with our economic state.[12] The most significant aspects of the issues of corporate and shareholder conduct, however, are policy questions which do not turn on the interpretation of legal rules.

An economic state has come into existence in which many activities of a public nature are attended by private instrumentalities. Corporations, their managers, their employees, and their shareholders are the main participants in that state. While corporation law may provide the constitutional structure of this economic state, governing the relationship of those interested in the corporation, this law is essentially permissive, consisting mainly of enabling statutes.[13] It does not give direction to the corporation. It is not corporation law which has molded an effective economic state; rather, that has been the function of private economic forces.[14] Indeed, corporation statutes may be devoid of any economic or social policy.[15]

This is not to suggest the irrelevancy of corporation law to the problems of the role of the corporation.[16] The law can, and does, have an important neutralizing effect. Corporation law can create the opportunity for socially responsible decisions to be made by eliminating impediments to those decisions. Thus, corporate managers are free as a result of the business judgment rule to decide to pursue socially responsible conduct as they deem appropriate and related to the best interest of the corporation.[17] Corporations are permitted to make charitable contributions,[18] indeed, there is even legal incentive to do so.[19] There is, however, no requirement under corporate law for managers to make socially responsible decisions or to make gifts to charities. The effect of the law is to allow managers to make these decisions free from the spectre of liability, but it does not impose liability on those who ignore the social side of corporate conduct, except as specifically mandated by regulatory legislation.

Thus, the major contribution of corporate law to the decision-making process has been in its avoidance of prepackaged answers, thereby allowing the resolution of decision-making problems to emerge out of considerations of social, political, and economic policy. The search for possible legal rules to express an emerging policy within the corporate constitutional arrangement will be fruitful if it compels one to think through the theoretical underpinnings of the corporation and its relation to society. Sound theory is necessary to deal with corporate problems rationally rather than as a response to the exercise of power.

Lawyers do more than just challenge corporate conduct, however. They also play an important role in shaping that conduct. The counselor of a large business enterprise possesses an influence which extends beyond furnishing opinions on technical legal questions. He is also involved as a policymaker. Significantly, his professional training at its best seeks to equip him to raise ethical questions, and consequently he is known to frequently question his client, management, about the appropriateness of its conduct.[20] Nothing has more sharply focused this issue than the role of lawyers in the post-Watergate revelations of corporate bribes and payoffs.

One has a feeling, supported by history, that if new corporate models or decision-making structures are to be devised to meet society's objectives for its economic functions, these structures will be shaped largely by lawyers. Lawyers are best trained to implement policy decisions that are constitutional in nature. Moreover, mechanical difficulties in implementing a proposal may render that idea—however laudable in concept—unworkable, and the lawyer's inclination to want to see how the details will work will require him to play a major role in shaping policy decisions.

The discussion that follows is not an outline of either existing or proposed black letter law, but consists rather of policy considerations. The points raised are intended to suggest some legal norms, which are offered for consideration both by lawyers and other framers of policy. They may prove useful in the formulation and execution of discretionary programs, as well as in those governed by the law.

Perspective and Prospective—A Dialectic

My own involvement in public interest proxy contests has impelled me to try to understand the direction of corporate policy. I can only offer some complex and ambivalent observations that are no more than tentative. Perhaps they can stimulate further contributions by way of rejoinder and exposure of the inevitable faults in this discussion.

The problems that have ignited the interest of social reformers in the corporation have not diminished, nor has the relationship of those problems to economic activity abated. As long as these basic facts remain, corporations will be challenged to act responsibly and the community will seek to bring this activity within its control.

The complexity of economic life requires the organization of our affairs through institutions, a course which has had the effect of separating people from direct control over their affairs. A power structure inevitably is created. Before changes are made in the existing power structure, and some changes may well be necessary, confidence is needed in the new arrangements. Philosophers and political scientists have long been concerned with the criteria for power and authority. Let me suggest one criterion that I think is appropriate in this particular context: Any arrangement must work effectively to produce sensible decisions at a cost that can be borne. Simply, this is a test of utility.

Cost in this sense must be read broadly to include the cost of external diseconomies that are borne by the entire community, such as polluted air and water, and those borne by special segments of the community, such as racial discrimination. This is a measurement of the corporate structure that tries to utilize economic analysis, since it is an economic function that is being evaluated.

The modern corporation confronts an identity crisis that would confound Freud. Some view the corporation as an instrument in a market economy, reacting only to market forces. Others see it as a quasi-political organization with a will to be exercised. The law is much concerned with power and its limitations. It sees the corporation as an entity which has legal rights and obligations. It has owners that are a constituency which delegates to others the right to exercise power. Thus, the law creates a model of corporate structure which appears like a pyramid, with shareholders at the base. A parliamentary analogy emerges, with the shareholders as the electorate, the board of directors as the legislature, and management (the chief officers and their principal technical advisors) as the cabinet.

This model, which clearly enhances shareholder democracy, is not, however, descriptive of the operations of most large corporations. There the board of directors usually is composed of management and outsiders selected by management. Management tends to be self-perpetuating, determining the goals of the corporation as if they were the owners. However, despite clear shortcomings in the model, at least operationally, some sort of structure is needed if the managers' power is to be kept within some definable limits. Management must be made accountable to someone, in accordance with a standard and by means of a process. The difficulty with this design is that shareholder democracy, which legitimizes management power, is not a functioning process.

Management has a schizophrenic attitude towards shareholder democracy. On one hand, they pay homage to the ritual and speak as if it functions. No doubt it behooves management to find that shareholder democracy has functioned wisely and well because it supports the legitimacy of the power of incumbent managers. While admiring the concept in form, however, management continually denies shareholders real participation in the decision-making process.

The Corporation and the Marketplace

Management is likely to perceive both the allocation of corporate power and the use of that power as governed not by the principles of democracy—or autocracy—but rather by the principles of the marketplace. Thus, investors register disagreement not with their votes, but by selling their shares. This is the Wall Street rule. It assumes that, if sufficient shareholders sell their stock in a negative reaction to management, the effect on the stock market is likely to produce a change in management through the "market for control."[21] Management is also likely to perceive that corporate activity, or the use of corporate power, is activated not by a political process but by prices and profits. Corporate decisions are undertaken on a cost-benefit analysis.

The virtues of the market model of decision making and allocation of power has its staunch defenders, notably Professors Milton Friedman and Henry Manne.[22] They urge that business leaders must follow the dictates of the marketplace, which they claim is strongly competitive, if capitalism is to function properly. As they see it, most of the problems which trouble the social reformers result from attempts to impede the marketplace by clumsy governmental regulation. They see shareholder democracy, as a governing model, to be irrelevant and, of course, nonexistent.

Professor Robert A. Dahl, a Yale political scientist, has described giant corporations as "political systems."[23] He views the corporate political system as an oligarchy, substantially unchecked by outside forces, including those of the market, stockholders, and the government.[24]

Synthesis and Coexistence

Where does this combination of fact and contention leave us? I believe there is a need for a corporate structure that will fulfill the criterion of utility outlined earlier. This structure must effectively work toward achieving society's goals at a tolerable cost. "Society's goals" embraces a range of wants too vast to detail here. One which is paramount, however, is the avoidance of excessively concentrated power in the hands of a few individuals—whether that power be concentrated in public or private hands. We seek popular control of our destiny. In my opinion, both the political and economic models for our corporations fall short of this criterion, although both models do contain functional elements. There is a need for synthesis of these elements, so as to enable the contending forces to co-exist and progress to be made. Accommodation is necessary for capitalism to survive, and I consider its survival to be a worthwhile goal.

Unlike a political state, the goals of any particular corporation are narrower in scope than the universe of society's concerns. This limitation makes managers more aware of proper corporate purposes and allows the corporation to perform its narrower function more effectively than a political body. The economic model of the corporation is the concept which renders it most efficient in achieving those goals. Its reliance on the market, with profits as a guide, maximizes free choice and avoids the greater danger of central planning. The problem with this model, as further discussion will show, is that it often imposes a high social cost on the community, rather than the corporation, to permit the latter to achieve its main goals. Moreover, this model may encourage the pursuit of goals that do not suit the long-term interest of the community, such as allowing corporate managers, acting within that economic model, to achieve great power. But, by and large, the economic notion of the corporation enables society to pursue effectively a central requirement of the community—the production of goods and services desired by its people.

Occasionally suggestions have been made to restructure corporations along the lines of the body politic. This suggestion presents some severe problems. In the first place, its implementation would be highly impractical. Who would vote? What mechanisms would govern the election?

The most rational suggestion for the political restructuring of the corporation has been advanced by Professor David L. Ratner.[25] In suggesting that shareholder voting be revised to provide one man-one vote, constituency groups would essentially choose themselves. That is, groups of citizens who felt that they had a sufficiently important stake in the corporate management could achieve this if enough members of that group bought a single share of stock and then voted themselves into control. Obviously, this is more easily said than done, a fact which would restrict its use to those with strong views, but perhaps its mere threat of success operates as a political restraint on management. That is, management would seek to avoid antagonizing citizen groups. The Ratner thesis is premised on a devout skepticism of the ability of corporate managers or institutional shareholders to produce more responsible corporate conduct[26] and, of course, on an inability to devise any other rational system of voting where citizens can have an impact.[27]

As to any proposal, we must question whether the undoubtedly high cost involved would produce commensurate benefits, and whether any proposal would be calculated to improve the quality of corporate decision making. We should also consider the effect on the capital market. Even if that market no longer occupies an important function in providing capital to business, as Berle argued,[28] it does serve as a governor on the management of many medium-sized corporations. Additionally, of course, 100 million persons have an important stake in the market that cannot be ignored.

It is in response to these questions that the politically structured corporation fails the test of utility. The argument that a corporation is political rests mainly on the contention that it affects many persons whether they choose to be affected or not. That effect comes about largely through the by-product of corporate activity. A corporation produces a product—its main task—and in the process pollutes the environment or refuses to employ minority group citizens— its by-product. Thus, the politically selected board would cause confusion in corporate goals, arising from the selection of decision makers whose primary concern is in dealing with the by-product in preference to the promotion of the main goal. Of course, there is no denying the need to deal with the by-product, but amelioration of the by-product is not the mission of the corporation, even though it is its responsibility. Thus, the main advantages of the corporation are lost by losing sight of its functions. Capital investors may feel the main brunt of that loss. Further, it stands to reason that there will be a loss of competence if managers are chosen by persons whose main interest is not to promote the growth of the corporation. The balancing of growth with the reduction of harmful effects is an increasingly complex problem that demands more, not less, competence.

A heavy toll of external diseconomies, ranging from pollution, discrimination, and impure and unsafe products, has been imposed upon society because the market structure as we know it implicitly encourages such conduct.[29] The ability of the market to function as a constraint demands more competition than prevails.[30] However, decisions made even in a perfectly functioning market place are made as individual decisions; the market is not a mechanism for group decisions but rather one for satisfying individual preferences. Consequently, the collective effect of individual judgments may be adverse to the community, especially to such nonparticipating members of the community as nonconsumers or small consumers. The community may suffer from what has been described as the "tyranny of small decisions."[31] Thus, while the individual choice in favor of a big car is made on the basis of one's own desires for a car, the accumulated effect may include the creation of a need for bigger highways. The collective decision to build those highways was predetermined by the smaller decisions that preceded it, which were made without regard for the cumulative effect. The collective decision that is thereby necessitated may not reflect the community's judgment as to what would be the wisest allocation of its resources, since there may have been little choice after the individual decisions were made. The result, when combined with the power of large corporations to shape demand, gives a quasi-political effect to the conduct of the large corporation. It is what prevents us from accepting the market—with nothing more—as the device for achieving society's economic goals.

The Moynihan View of the Market

In addition to these imperfections and distortions, Daniel P. Moynihan has pointed out another aspect of the market.[32] He gives full credit to the strengths and achievements of capitalism, but notes Schumpeter's view that capitalism will provide its own undoing. Moynihan observes that there are many values that comprise the general welfare. Economic welfare is only one of these. But the market function, by necessity, insensitizes itself to those other interests and to those who "assert a notion of general welfare which on occasion requires some modification, even restraint in the pursuit of economic welfare."[33] To illustrate his point, Moynihan recounts the experience of the automobile industry in withstanding pressures for safety improvements. This was accomplished not by the companies' oligopolistic position, which permitted the imposition of their will on the consumer, but rather by the fact that management had so identified itself with the consumer that their thinking was identical. Since consumers preferred not to think about safety and crashes, management spurned it as well. Moynihan concludes that "the difficulty is simply that a mind attuned to the market place acquires an almost trained insensitivity to nonmarket considerations." He then adds, "[t]he task of liberalism is to provide the economic system with this missing component."[34]

Some will see in this a failure of capitalism since neither political nor economic models can function effectively within the capitalist framework. Perhaps it is true, as Moynihan speculates, that eventually we will have the kind of economic centralization "generally associated with the term socialism."[35] He also sees that "corporate responsibility is a device whereby modern liberalism is seeking to save capitalism from itself."[36] Moynihan's comment that political democracy rarely exists under other economic systems explains why it is worth the effort to seek the solution to our problems within the system.

Consequently, numerous industry leaders have implored other businessmen to seek wider goals for business. Dan Lufkin, a former investment banker and one of the most outspoken advocates of this position, sees the need as critical. He fears that "the corporation may be dying because its cold, implacable power is unacceptable in a world where humanity itself is struggling to survive. The corporation can no longer hold itself aloof from society, nor can the corporate manager measure his success solely in terms of costs cut or profits maximized."[37] The sentiments are expressed by many individuals and by groups of businessmen.[38]

Commendable as it may be, voluntary good citizenship by corporate managers under a profit-oriented system will not work effectively.[39] If full responsibility to deal with the wide range of social problems is entrusted to corporate managers, we would incur the great danger that corporations would fail in all of their functions, owing to a lack of adequate standards to guide managers. From the community's standpoint, it is inadequate to rely too much on such voluntarism to deal with society's problems, since corporate management, as we know it, has neither the training nor the desire to discharge these broader tasks. Thus, the necessary balance between profit functions and noneconomic goals of society cannot be left to well-intentioned management alone.

The answer that government should guard against those externalities caused by the market place and should protect otherwise unrepresented interests is true, of course, but it is also insufficient. It is not that government regulation is not valuable, but it has a high rate of failure. Government as a protector of the public from the power of large corporation tends to be defective. Some government regulation is designed to create a cartel and protect large corporations from competition. The regulation of transportation is a prime example.[40] But even where government regulation is designed to constrain corporate power, its agencies are often immobilized as the regulated assume control of the regulatory forces.

If reliance on the good intention of managers and on government proves inadequate in the achievement of our synthesis, we should examine other institutionalized means of producing the desired result. One method might be through the market mechanism. By adding costs to the type of conduct we wish to discourage and by providing rewards for conduct we seek to encourage, we might effectively force managers to direct business more in the service of our entire society. In other words, our pricing system should reflect those social priorities that are presently ignored. Taxes, credits, and new accounting concepts may be needed. The use of market mechanisms has been suggested as the means to deal with such varied social problems as automobile accidents[41] and population control.[42]

The influence of the market to promote social goals, however, cannot occur without governmental interference. This means a willingness by politically powerful forces to accept change. Among other requirements, steps to invigorate competition and control or reduce the powerful influence of dominant market forces are needed. The fear that, unless they do so, worse will happen might achieve a begrudging acceptance.

Thus, a political climate which insists that serving the public interest is a pre-condition to being allowed to pursue profit-oriented goals might instill such fear and serve as a potentially powerful incentive—comparable to a market mechanism—for corporations to find methods of achieving social goals. Social activism—such as the efforts of Ralph Nader—are an invaluable institutional tool in compelling corporate responsibility. Public relations campaigns conducted by business seem to fully appreciate this point as an increasingly greater effort is made to persuade the public and politicians that business, through voluntary acts, is serving the public interest. If we appreciate the fact that voluntarism is not sufficient, management may find that it is a business imperative to institutionalize methods to understand the public interest so as to be able to serve it and to avoid the ultimate cost of loss of private freedom. This apocalyptic analysis may not be likely, but neither can it be ignored.

Thus, we must reject the restructuring of the corporation into a political model, since the cost to revise the structure would excessively impair the effectiveness of the corporation. We have not, however, rejected the need for management to broaden its horizons.[43] In achieving this goal, improvement in the process of shareholder democracy would prove useful.

It would be helpful to begin by accepting the notion that there is a legitimate and necessary shareholder concern and responsibility with the social impact of corporate conduct. The next step is to explore methods whereby shareholder democratic forms can be related to turn corporate conduct in a more responsible direction. This responsibility would rest largely upon what has been called the "Kew Gardens Principle," recalling the murder of Kitty Genovese in Kew Gardens in 1964 while 38 people watched or heard and refused to get involved. Shareholders, like the 38 witnesses, confront a situation where there is a need for action, there is a proximity to the situation, they possess the capability to act, and they are the last resort.[44]

Recognition of the responsibility, even just viewing it as an opportunity, would be desirable as it would tend to increase the interest within the community about those things that affect it. Perhaps it would counter the growing "atrophy of responsibility already pervasive in a highly organized society."[45] Most shareholders are likely to abdicate any responsibility to management. Some, notably institutions taking a broad perspective of their overall purpose, will not. Their persuasive force could prove useful in convincing management to adopt different policies and practices on their own initiative.

The enlivening process entails giving wide latitude to shareholders to take action on matters of public policy. Clearly, this must be done through the proxy process and particularly with the aid of a liberal interpretation, or possibly revision, of the shareholder proposal rule. Perhaps more importantly, however, shareholders should be entitled to receive more information about the enterprise, including information relating to matters of social concern. The foregoing argument would suggest that the scope of information required to be furnished should not be limited exclusively to data which has profit implications but should include details bearing upon social questions.[46] Of course, the two are frequently intertwined. Further, the election process itself should be improved to provide a genuine opportunity for interested shareholders to participate. Self-perpetuation should not be guaranteed; increased general access to the proxy machinery is in order.[47] These matters involve both federal and state law at the present time. While federal law could have specified the areas on which shareholders can vote, the appropriateness of voting is left to state law. The shareholder's right to obtain information is primarily a matter of state law. Reform of the law to enlarge the shareholder role, however, could proceed along either federal or state lines.

Another step in improving the corporate apparatus would be to institutionalize an effective self-criticism process. Its value was best expressed in a significant speech by former SEC Chairman Manuel F. Cohen, in which he raised questions concerning the legitimacy of corporate power. Cohen stated that the exercise of corporate power "must be subject to free and systematic analysis and criticism," and added:

Those within industry need to hear all the competing arguments if they are to form a balanced judgment about their long term interests, the interests of their industry and of the economy which gives them sustenance. Otherwise, they may only see a very narrow, often transient, and quite possibly a self-defeating view of self-interest. The individual business leader, no matter how clever or well intentioned, does not always see all the consequences of his decisions. Like all of us in government, he is fallible, and can learn from others. He also has another very human characteristic. Like all of us, he doesn't always take kindly to criticism.

That is why I always stress the need for *institutionalized* procedure designed to protect, promote free analysis and criticism of business, as well as governmental, decisions as they affect the community. The press can help in the realization of this goal.[48]

The search for self-critical mechanisms should also consider the use or adaptability of several foreign models. Thus, some German[49] and Swedish[50] corporations have boards which include representatives designated by government. A French commentator, Francois Bloch-Laine, has suggested that corporations could be subjected to the surveillance of an independent magistrature who would look after the affairs of particular businesses and verify whether the corporation had met its obligations to shareholders, employees, and the public.[51] Conceivably, none of these devices may prove workable, and it is premature to urge their immediate adoption by American corporations. They are, however, worthy of further careful study and consideration.

Improved Disclosure

The final suggestion for improving and widening the decision-making process is through improved disclosure. The impact of corporate decisions on the public generally escapes public notice. For example, little detailed information is available concerning corporate discrimination and pollution. Obviously, some information must be protected but probably not as much as management claims.

Shareholders need pertinent information about the impact of corporate decisions and not just for the purpose of being able to decide whether earnings or stock prices will be affected. Rather, since the shareholders' position in management's election is what legitimizes management's power, shareholders should be able to make decisions on the basis of adequate information before they make themselves part of the process. Institutions that are concerned with public welfare should be especially mindful of this relationship.[52]

There is also a great indirect value involved in the disclosure of this kind of information. Disclosure can work like a market mechanism. The disclosure of unflattering information imposes a cost—the cost of embarrassment—which might quickly turn into the cost of consumer retaliation. To avoid paying that cost, companies would have to change the facts required to be disclosed should they be embarrassing. Thus, disclosure could lead to the employment of more blacks, the abatement of pollution, or the production of safer automobiles so as to avoid recall.

There is a valuable disclosure lesson to be learned from a vivid political analogy. Even a politically democratic government, like that of the United States, can turn against its people when it is able to operate without requirement of full disclosure.[53] The publication of the Pentagon Papers reveals how much a government was able to get away with while operating in secrecy. And, of course, Watergate is a monument to tragic, surreptitious conduct which had its counterpart in executive suites. The National Environmental Policy Act of 1969 declares it to be a national policy to use all practicable means to foster an improved environment and requires federal agencies to review their policies and procedures so as to bring them into line with the Act. The SEC does not see the promotion of these goals as part of its mission, and its action has been limited to requiring disclosure of environmental impact that has a clear profit impact.[54]

This is a myopic response because it too narrowly views the data necessary for complete evaluation of the company, and because it is a rejection of the most important device available for the government to further an important social objective. It is a needlessly narrow concept of the role of the SEC, which is charged not only with the protection of investors but with the protection of the public interest.[55] The SEC should search for ways to define clearly what must be disclosed and to develop understandable requirements that a court can enforce, rather than look for reasons not to do so. Thus, private enforcement can furnish the necessary enforcement supplement.

Federal Corporation Law

Part of the strength of corporate management is an outgrowth of our federal system. A corporation may be formed under the laws of any state and can qualify to do business in all others. As a resident of the state of its incorporation, its internal affairs will be governed by the laws of that state, and it will pay taxes to that state. Thus, the states have some incentive to attract incorporation business.[56]

The decision of where to incorporate is made by corporate managers, and, therefore, state law tries to lure business by appealing to the managers' own interests. Charter mongering has been a going business since the 1870s when New Jersey imaginatively amended its laws to appeal to the growing number of corporations. However, Delaware has dominated the incorporation field since it amended its statute in 1899.[57] Through the years the statute has been amended continually in order to maintain that position.[58] Thus, Delaware law allows wide flexibility to management, provides generous indemnification provisions, permits the abolition of the annual meeting, and simply refuses to enact provisions that would seriously restrict managers.[59]

This is not the occasion to examine in depth the wisdom or the specifics of a federal corporation statute.[60] It might be helpful, however, to set forth the general aims described for federal corporation law and to suggest areas where particular study will be needed.

It is necessary to think systematically about a corporate statute in order to properly evaluate the concept of a federal corporation law. The proposal is a significant departure from our federal system, and that necessarily raises some constitutional questions. Existing corporate charters are contracts protected by the Constitution. While the state has power to amend its laws to apply retroactively to existing corporations, it is another question as to whether federal law could undo those arrangements. Federal chartering could apply prospectively only and avoid that problem. Such a federal law would be meaningless, however, if it were to leave unaffected existing corporations. State laws could be left unaffected and federal law superimposed as an additional requirement, but that kind of federal law would have to affect existing arrangements that are embodied in state law to achieve its objectives. If federal law were offered as only an alternative to state law, it would probably be rejected unless it was weaker than state law. If weaker, it would fail in its objectives.[61]

In addition, a plan for corporate structure might have to be spelled out in the statute. Thus, if popularization of the corporation is desired—itself a major question—what devices will be created to achieve it? The occasion for writing the statutes is when we would have to stop speaking in generalities about this proposition and spell out the details. Presumably, we would then have to weigh the cost against the benefits. There are other important questions concerning the governing structure such as the role of the board of directors, the corporate functions reserved to the shareholder body, requirements for shareholder meetings, and cumulative voting.

State laws presently provide diverse answers with respect to financial and accounting questions. A federal law might force us to make a choice in an area where uniformity may not be needed. State law has begun to recognize and distinguish between the needs of close corporations and those of publicly held corporations. Will a federal statute sweep up the close corporation within its scope and provide a regulatory approach where the main advance has probably been the expansion of permissiveness?

What device will be used to administer this statute? Visions of a mammoth bureaucracy come to mind, with fears of inefficiency, lack of imagination, and concentration and abuse of power. Many additional substantive questions are involved that are presently dealt with by regulatory legislation. Included are questions of disclosure and antitrust. Would there be any improvement over the regulatory scheme by placing these functions under a federal incorporation law? Likewise, another of Nader's concerns—increased individual accountability—has been proposed by the National Commission of Reform of the Federal Criminal Laws through existing structures.[62]

There is a basic attraction in concept of a federal incorporation law. It seems anomolous to have a single small state determine the law governing the affairs of multibillion, multinational corporations when such internal rules have effects on millions of citizens. Should Delaware rule the world? This question is especially appropriate since the effect of that approach has been to give vast power to private power centers, only ineffectually held accountable to the public. Thus, it is worth the intellectual effort to see if improvements can be made in the present scheme. Frustration with state, judge-made law has encouraged federal corporate common law principally in the area of management's fiduciary duties, and that has created a higher standard of conduct. Clearly, this would be a politically difficult proposal to adopt. But one of the many important benefits to be derived from the study would be that very significant problems would get exposure, fundamental questions about our economy would be asked, and all in a forum where the power exists to do something about it.[63]

Conclusion

This article stops short of recommending the political transformation of our corporate structure. I believe that what is needed is an attempt to balance our problems and the use of our resources. Certainly, problems that grow out of business policy and activity are severe, but we need continued economic activity as well as new priorities. Rather than politicize the corporate structure, it is recommended that market mechanisms be found to shape corporate conduct towards society's overall goals and that efforts be made to broaden corporate thinking in that direction. For this purpose, it is suggested that the corporate democratic forms be invigorated, that management discover self-critical mechanisms, and that greater disclosure of corporate social conduct be required.

Potential solutions to our problems should be explored in the context of examining federal incorporation. The result of all this might be a broader decision-making base and de facto accountability of corporate managers to those that they affect, which is important if we are ever to harmonize our economic activity with society's idea of general welfare.

It is risky to ignore the political climate and dynamics in which these questions arise. Leaders in government and business have often put aside the emotional appeals of social critics as merely the traditional protests of youth. They remember their own days of protest. I think, however, that it may be a serious miscalculation to equate the protests of the 1970s with those of the past. Such an error could cause changes far more tumultuous than those being suggested. The persistence of interest in corporate responsibility should be a reminder that we do not have much leisure to debate social and economic reform. This is not stated as a threat—it is a plea, uttered with regret.

Notes

1. Berle, "Corporate Powers as Powers in Trust," 44 *Harv. L. Rev.* 1049 (1931); Berle, "For Whom Corporate Managers Are Trustees: A Note," 45 *Har.*

L. Rev. 1365 (1932); Dodd, "For Whom Are Corporate Managers Trustees?" 45 Harv. L. Rev. 1145 (1932); Dodd, "Is Effective Enforcement of the Fiduciary Duty of Corporate Managers Practicable?" 2 U. Chi. L. Rev. 194 (1935).

2. See A.P. Smith Mfg. Co. v. Barlow, 13 N.J. 145, 98 A.2d 581, *appeal dismissed*, 346 U.S. 861 (1953); Note, "Corporate Altruism: A Rational Approach," 59 *Geo. L. J.* 117 (1970).

3. See Statement of Owen D. Young, President of General Electric Co., in 1929, *quoted in* W. Cary, *Cases and Materials on Corporations*, 239-40 (4th ed. 1969).

4. The corporate responsibility movement has been described as potentially "the most significant political development of the 1970's." See Henderson, "Politics by Other Means," *The Nation*, Dec. 14, 1970, p. 617.

5. See *Austin Report* 2. A similar recommendation is made in Simon, Powers & Gunneman, *The Ethical Investor* (1971). See also Malkiel & Quandt, "Moral Issues in Investment Policy," *Harv. Bus. Rev.*, Mar.-Apr. 1971, p. 37.

6. See discussion of the Dreyfus Third Century Fund, note 52 *infra* and accompanying text. None of the "social responsibility" funds has thrived, it should be noted.

7. See 5 *SEC Institutional Investor Study* 2720.

8. Id., p. 2533.

9. See Malkiel & Quandt, *supra* note 5, p. 41.

10. See 5 *SEC Institutional Investor Study* 2753-55. A spokesman for the Bank of America was reported as saying: "[W]e hold stock for investment purposes, and to vote against management would be inconsistent with that purpose." *The Wall Street Journal*, Apr. 28, 1971, p. 1, col. 6.

According to letters sent to the Project on Corporate Responsibility, some banks forwarded proxies to the principal if important or unusual issues were involved, but others voted in accordance with their own judgment.

One unusual instance last spring involved the proxy contest at Midas International Corp. The challenger held a substantial bloc in trust, and he requested the bank to vote those shares in his favor. The bank refused, thereby defeating the attempted take-over bid. See *Time*, May 3, 1971, p. 84.

11. See *Austin Report* 3-4. In a book growing out of a Yale University seminar, the conclusion was reached that the responsibility for university decision making must rest with the trustees, and that "plenary involvement of the university community in investment decisions should be minimized or excluded." Simon, Powers & Gunnemann, *supra* note 5.

12. See A. Berle & G. Means, *The Modern Corporation and Private Property* 357 (1932).

13. See Latty, "Why are Business Corporation Laws Largely 'Enabling?' " 50 *Cornell L. Q.* 599 (1965).

14. W. Hurst, *The Legitimacy of the Business Corporation in the Law of the United States* 10-11 (1970).

15. See Comments by B. Manning in *Economic Policy and the Regulation of Corporate Securities* 81 (H. Manne ed. 1969).

16. Obviously, substantive law in other areas has a great deal to do with the shaping of corporate policy, such as antitrust law, securities law, labor law, tax law, equal employment opportunity law, and environmental protection law. The singularity of corporation law is that it is the body of law concerned with the internal structure of the corporate entity—its constitutional aspects—and it is the body of law that equips the corporation with the legal apparel that gives it its distinctiveness.

17. See N. Lattin, *Corporations* 211-12 (2d ed. 1971). See also Blumberg, "Corporate Responsibility and the Social Crisis," 50 *B.U.L. Rev.* 157 (1970); Schwartz, "The Public Interest Proxy Contest: Reflections on Campaign GM," 69 *Mich. L. Rev.* 419, 472 (1971).

18. See *Del. Code Ann.* tit. 8, §122(a) (1953); *ABA-ALI Model Bus. Corp. Act* §4(m) (1960).

19. See *Int. Rev. Code of 1954*, §170.

20. Judge Charles E. Wyzanski has observed:

The modern lawyer almost invariably advises his client not only on what is permissible, but also what is desirable. And it is in the public interest that the lawyer should regard himself as more than a predictor of legal consequences. His duty to society as well as to his client involves many relevant social, economic, political, and philosophical considerations.

United States v. United Shoe Machinery Corp., 89 F. Supp. 357, 359 (D. Mass. 1950). See E. Smigel, *The Wall Street Lawyer* 6 (1964); Mayer, "Keepers of the Business Conscience," *Harpers*, Feb. 1956, pp. 50, 55.

21. See Manne, "Good for General Motors?" *Barron's,* May 18, 1970, p. 8; Manne, "Mergers and the Market for Corporate Control," 73 *J. Pol. Econ.* 110 (1965).

22. See Friedman, "The Social Responsibility of Business is to Increase its Profits," *N.Y. Times*, Sept. 13, 1970, §6 (magazine), p. 32; Manne, "The Myth of Corporate Responsibility," 26 *Bus. Law.* 533 (1970). See also P. Heyne, *Private Keepers of the Public Interest* (1968).

23. R. Dahl, *After the Revolution?* (1970).

24. Dahl contends that under the principle of affected interests, "citizenship" in the corporation cannot be given to shareholders alone when employees and customers also make a vital contribution to the firm. Therefore, the "privileged" status of the shareholders is anachronistic. Moreover, ownership of the large corporation has in fact been separated from control, and therefore there is no longer any reason to link citizenship with the right to receive profits.

25. See Ratner, "The Government of Business Corporations: Critical Reflections on the Rule of 'One Share, One Vote,'" 56 *Cornell L. Rev.* 1 (1970).

26. Id., p. 24.
27. Id., p. 33.
28. See Berle, Introduction to A. Berle & G. Means, *The Modern Corporation and Private Property* (rev. ed. 1969). But see Lintner, "The Financing of Corporations," in *The Corporation in Modern Society* 166 (Mason ed. 1966).
29. See Kapp, *The Social Costs of Private Enterprise* (paperback ed. 1971).
30. Recent expositions on the lack of competitiveness in the market include M. Mintz & J. Cohen, *America, Inc.* (1971) and *The Closed Enterprise System* (M. Green ed. 1971).
31. See Kahn, "The Tyranny of Small Decisions: Failures, Imperfections and the Limits of Economics," 19 *Kyklos* 23 (1966); W. Baumol, *Enlightened Self-Interest and Corporate Philanthropy in a New Rationale for Corporate Social Policy* 16 (Comm. for Economic Development pamphlet 1970). Similarly, Samuelson notes the "fallacy of competition" and states that what is good for individuals is not always good for society. P. Samuelson, *Economics* 12 (8th ed. 1970).
32. See Address by Daniel P. Moynihan, Arthur K. Solomon Lecture, New York Univ. School of Bus., Apr. 26, 1971.
33. Id. p. 27.
34. Id. p. 43.
35. Id. p. 23.
36. Id. p. 26.
37. Address by Dan W. Lufkin to members of the Connecticut Council of the New England Council, Sept. 22, 1970; address by Dan W. Lufkin to Harvard Business School Club of New York, Nov. 18, 1970.
38. See Committee for Economic Development, *Social Responsibilities of Business Corporations* (1971), cited in *N.Y. Times,* July 1, 1971, p. 71, col. 4. See generally Henderson, "Toward Managing Social Conflict," *Harv. Bus. Rev.*, May-June 1971, p. 82. Evidence has also been furnished to show that good management achieves a harmony of profit and other goals. The companies in the pulp and paper industry that were highly rated by the Council on Economic Priorities with regard to pollution control were shown, in a paper by Joseph H. Bragdon and John A. Marlin, to have the best earnings record during 1965-1971, and the lowest ranked by the Council on Economic Priorities was one of the least profitable. One conclusion suggested by Bragdon and Marlin is that good management is good business.
39. Cf. Neil Chamberlain, *The Limits of Corporate Responsibility* (1974).
40. See M. Mintz & J. Cohen, *supra* note 30, p. 248; Cordtz, "It's Time to Unload the Regulators," *Fortune,* July 1971, p. 64.
41. See generally G. Calabresi, *The Costs of Accidents: A Legal and Economic Analysis* (1970).
42. See generally Note, "Legal Analysis and Population Control: The Problem of Coercion," 84 *Harv. L. Rev.* 1856 (1971).

43. See R. Likert, *The Influence of Social Research on Corporate Responsibility in a New Rationale for Corporate Social Policy* 20 (Comm. for Economic Development pamphlet 1970), a broader based decision-making structure makes for better business decisions.

44. See Simon, Powers & Gunnemann, *supra* note 5. See also A. Hirschman, *Exit, Voice and Loyalty* (1970).

45. Simon, Powers & Gunnemann, *supra* note 5.

46. The SEC's position is to deem information "material" within the meaning of securities laws only insofar as there is a discernible relationship to profit. SEC Securities Act Releases No. 5627 (Oct. 14, 1975) and No. 5704 (May 6, 1976).

47. See Eisenberg, "Access to the Corporate Proxy Machinery," 83 *Harv. L. Rev.* 1489 (1970).

48. Address by Manuel F. Cohen, Chairman SEC, to the Economic Club of Detroit, Jan. 27, 1969 (transcript, pp. 9-10).

49. See generally Steefel & Falkenhausen, "The New German Stock Corporation Law," 52 *Cornell L.Q.* 518, 537-39 (1937); Vagts, "Reforming the 'Modern' Corporation: Perspectives from the German," 80 *Harv. L. Rev.* 23, 42, 80-81 (1966).

50. See *N.Y. Times*, Feb. 1, 1971, p. 45, col. 2.

51. See A. Shonfield, *Modern Capitalism*, 381-82 (Oxford Paperback ed., 1965).

52. One such institution, the Dreyfus Third Century Fund, organized in 1971, describes its investment policy as follows:

It is the intention of the management of the fund to limit its selection of investments to securities of those companies which, in the opinion of management, show leadership or progress in the areas of, or have demonstrated their concerns for the protection and improvement of, the environment and proper use of the nation's natural resources, consumer and occupational safety, product purity and its effect on the environment; equal employment opportunity, the health, education, and housing demands of America, or in other areas which help to improve the quality of life in the United States. It is also the intention of the management of the Fund to eliminate from its portfolio the securities that, in the opinion of management, cease to meet these criteria for the Fund's portfolio selections.

See The Dreyfus Third Century Fund, Inc., Preliminary Prospectus, May 7, 1971, p. 3. The Pax Fund, organized by the United Methodist Church, and Social Dimensions Fund, formed by Pennsylvania Mutual Fund manager Ralph Quinter, strive for similar objectives. See *Bus. Week*, Sept. 4, 1971, p. 56.

53. A great journalist, Joseph Pulitzer, once observed:

We are a democracy, and there is only one way to get a democracy on its feet in the matter of its individual, its social, its municipal, its State, its National conduct, and that is by keeping the public informed about what is going on. There is not a crime, there is not a dodge, there is not a trick, there is not a swindle, there is not a vice which does not live by secrecy. Get these things out in the open, describe them, attack them, ridicule them in the press, and sooner or later public opinion will sweep them away.

Publicity may not be the only thing that is needed, but it is the one thing without which all other agencies will fail.

W. Swanberg, *Pulitzer* 402-03 (1967).

54. See SEC Securities Act Releases No. 5170 (July 19, 1971), No. 5386 (April 20, 1973), and No. 5704 (May 6, 1976).

55. See Sonde & Pitt, "Utilizing the Federal Securities Laws to 'Clear the Air! Clean the Sky! Wash the Wind!' " 16 *How. L.J.* 83 (1971).

56. See Kaplan, "Foreign Corporations and Local Corporate Policy," 21 *Vand. L. Rev.* 433 (1968).

57. As of Jan. 4, 1965, 433 of the 1250 corporations listed on the New York Stock Exchange were incorporated in Delaware. New York was in second place with 164 corporations. Id. p. 435 n.5.

58. See Note, "Law for Sale: A Study of the Delaware Corporation Law of 1967," 117 *U. Pa. L. Rev.* 861 (1969).

59. See W. Cary, "Federalism and Corporate Law: Reflections Upon Delaware," 83 *Yale L.J.* 663 (1974).

60. See R. Nader, M. Green, J. Seligson, *Taming the Giant Corporation*, (1976); Schwartz, "A Case for Federal Chartering of Corporations," 31 *Bus. Lawyer* 1125 (1976).

61. See Berlack, "Federal Incorporation and Securities Regulations," 49 *Harv. L. Rev.* 394, 404 (1936); Note, "Federal Chartering of Corporations: Constitutional Challenges," 62. *Geo. L. J.* 123 (1972).

62. See BNA Sec. Reg. & L. Rep., No. 93, p. B-1 (Mar. 17, 1971).

63. Hearings on this subject were held by the Senate Commerce Committee in June 1976, and the collected views are indeed a valuable source of information. U.S. Senate, *Corporate Rights and Responsibilities*, 1976.

6-3 Sinful Structures: Society and Education

Robert J. Henle, S.J.

We have heard a great deal about "sinful" structures from activists and from revolutionary theologians. The extreme student activists of the late 60s and early 70s were particularly violent and virulent in condemning all our social and political structures as sinful. No matter that they were unable to think beyond the point when our society's organization would be completely dismantled and we would exist simply as a vast mob of individuals.

They seemed to know little of history and to have no imaginative realization of the overwhelming amount of human suffering a successful total revolution entails. We know what havoc a prolonged blackout, a great flood or a race riot can wreak, but we have no large historical experience of total revolution. Anarchy frees every scoundrel and blackguard to enrich and empower himself through the suffering of ordinary people, who are defenseless in the universal disorder. Even the oppressed, once released, can become as brutal and vindictive as their oppressors. Almost always the new structures—often dictatorial—seem little better than the original sinful ones and hardly worth the final cost in human degradation and misery. The tragedy of Lebanon is a small and limited example of violent social disruption.

That we in the U.S. are a "revolutionary people" in the activist sense is simply false. Our revolution was the separation of one society from another. The political organs and social instrumentalities of the colonies remained fairly intact during the American revolution.

A Clarification of Terms

To determine our attitude toward a society or any one of its structures requires objectivity, balanced judgment, and clear thinking. The very use of the term, sinful, to describe structures obfuscates thinking and skews the issues. I strongly object to this abuse of language and thought. Structures cannot be truly sinful; sin lies in the human will, not in anything outside the soul. Saint Thomas and other moralists emphatically distinguish the just as objective and as objectively distinguishable from the virtuous internal act of justice and the sinful internal act of injustice. Arrangements, laws, external actions, structures can be just or unjust, they cannot be sinful. I am not dealing in niceties of language or in scholastic quibbles. It is of capital importance for any evaluation of society and for the study of justice to insist on this distinction.[1] No doubt one can rhetorically transfer sinful to structures if one wishes to arouse mindless emotions, but this use handicaps sober judgment and does violence to language itself.

Before continuing, it is important to note that a *just society*, complete and perfect, has never and will never exist. It is an inspiring ideal, but we must often not only settle for, but support the second best. In social practice as elsewhere the "best" is often the enemy of the "good." In the first place a just society would presuppose total control by completely just men. The ancient Greek Pittakos was content to call a *polis* just "if it is not possible for the wicked to rule ... and if it is likewise not possible for the good to be excluded from ruling ..."[2]

In addition to possessing the virtue of justice, just rulers must be assumed to have adequate political and technological skills to devise a system (structure) that will, for the most part, operate to a just result. Philosophers of law have recognized that even the best set of laws cannot realize a constant level of uniform justice; an open-ended discretionary corrective called "equity" (*epieikeia*) is necessary to remedy the defects of any legal system. Certainly no group of men—just or unjust—possesses knowledge adequate to arrange modern social, economic, legal, and political complexities into an efficient and just whole. For this reason also we shall have to live with imperfection.

It should be noted at this point that the unjust can exist in a structure or system without there being necessarily any personal guilt or sin. In fact, some systems devised with the best will in the world have turned out to be shot through with injustice. The U.S. welfare system—good on the whole—may be just such a system. I am saying that welfare itself is a good idea in our society, but its administration reflects the frustrating impersonalism of our society. If mistreated under a well-intentioned system, the frustrated victim has no one on whom to vent his rage; this increases his feelings of impotence.

Another prenote is necessary. Structures must not be reified; they do not act or operate, they do not of themselves always and automatically produce just or unjust results. Structures no doubt have a determining influence on human actions, especially in the case of routine activities of minor officials, bureaucrats, or clerks in agencies and courts. But men also manage and manipulate structures. Intelligent, courageous, and just men can turn imperfect systems toward good and can find ways to mitigate evil effects. On the other hand, weak or evil men can use or abuse just structures in ways that promote injustice. A good example here might be in the incredible acts of some of Germany's most respected judges under the Nazi regime.

The full classical meaning of *justice* includes as its subject matter directly or indirectly all relationships between men.[3] Generally, these relationships are classified in three major groupings:

1. The relations of individuals to one another.
2. The relations of the society or community (not merely the state) to individuals.
3. The relations of individuals to the whole society or community.

We speak thus of commutative justice, of social justice, and of legal justice (or general justice). The just rectitude of any society includes the rectitude of all these patterns of relationships.

The Complexity of Modern Injustice

If we now attempt an overview of the measure of justice in world society or in U.S. society, the enormous complexity of society makes the effort incredibly difficult. No society in the history of the world has ever reached the size and complexity, the pluralism and diversity of society in the United States. If we could romantically quantify all this, we would have to *multiply* the size by the complexity to reach an index of the difficulty of analysis. In the United States there are over 200 million persons to be interrelated, each in a variety of ways. (No society ever provided so many roles for its members as does ours. How simple seems the role of the Athenian gentleman in the *polis* of Pericles' day!) Just in the business world alone there are more than 9 million solo business enterprises, 900,000 partnerships and 1,600,00 corporations.[4] To evaluate the level of the just in U.S. society seems impossible; to establish indices of justice seems beyond human capacity.

Yet there are some overall tests. Violence is always a sign of injustice: It is either a simple unjust act (as in murder), a justified use of appropriate force against unjust acts, or an exaggerated and unjust reaction against injustice. By the index of violence, world society and U.S. society, especially U.S. urban society, are indeed unjust and increasingly so. Some have exaggerated this aspect of society to the point of calling us one of the most violent peoples in all history. I do not share this view, but I understand it. A more discriminating index discloses that much of this violence is against the innocent, the defenseless, the weak, and the poor. For example, a recent poll indicates that the number-one worry of urban elderly people is fear of mugging, assault, robbery, and personal violence.

Another common index is the relative distribution of material goods. Already in ancient times Thales (640?-546 B.C.) said, "If there is neither excessive wealth nor immoderate poverty in a nation, then justice may be said to prevail."[5] Saint Thomas continues this view: "... avarice is a sin directly against neighbor because with material possessions it is impossible for one man to enjoy extreme wealth without someone else suffering extreme want..."[6]

It would appear that Western industrialized societies have produced through their own prosperity and growth not only men of incredible individual wealth or control of wealth (the late Mr. Getty's estate is an obscene share in the world's wealth), but also and regularly (not only during recessions) groups of miserable, depressed, and hopeless people, especially in the hearts of our cities and in impoverished rural areas. I have heard distinguished economists say that the industrialization (that is, the progress) of the third-world countries is producing (and the more it progresses will continue to produce) greater misery among the lowest 20 percent of the socioeconomic classes.[7] Societies which *per se* produce such human misery and do not *per accidens* provide humane correction must have a degree of injustice built into their structures.

Another index of injustice might be the increasing incidence of man-made disasters with long-term horrendous effects. The recent dioxin explosion in Italy may turn hundreds of fertile acres into a desert for years to come. The kepone tragedy in Virginia may destroy the recreational and commercial value of Chesapeake Bay. Less spectacular is the almost permanent destruction of topsoil by strip mining; less long term is the failure of the Teton River Dam in Idaho and of the dam at Buffalo Creek in West Virginia. In this latter case some 600 plaintiffs recovered some $13 million in damages, but the damages do not replace dead mothers and fathers or destroyed and washed away homes and farms.

A terrible fear is spreading through all industrial areas. Are we creating hundreds of industrial and technological open-ended time bombs and even booby-trapping our homes?[8] I have a little tube of permanent adhesive which carries horrendous warnings:

DANGER! EXTREMELY FLAMMABLE MIXTURE
Keep product and its vapors away from heat, sparks and open flames. Use in well ventilated areas. Avoid eye contact and prolonged or repeated contact with the skin. Cleanse skin with nail polish remover. For eye contact, flush immediately with plenty of water and seek medical aid. Keep out of reach of children. Keep container closed when not in use. Do not drip on finished surfaces.

What of the factories and men making this stuff?! Any society that is so organized as to permit (and promote?) disasters of this caliber cannot be a just society.

A more public and widely disturbing index is the disclosure of appalling dishonesty and lack of integrity among our top leadership. Watergate is, of course, the most obvious, trite, and frightening example; but other disclosures of bribery, illegal collusion, callous selfishness in the highest levels of business corporations are equally revealing. We can add the disregard of ethics by professional men in medicine and law. Here we have Pittakos' test: the rule (control and power) of unjust and wicked men. In these cases the wickedness of leaders and the potentialities for evil in our structures combine to destroy the basic justice of our society. In sum, these indices, since they are general and recurrent, indicate the existence of systematic or structural injustice.

Now, while we can conclude from these and other indices that our society is indeed unjust, we must balance this by acknowledging that our institutions do realize a great deal of justice and that there is in our society a strong drive toward justice. We have to face the difficult task of examining our society structure by structure, individually and in relation to each other; then the more difficult task of determining how to correct or improve deficient systems, structures, and institutions must be faced. A blanket condemnation of our society is as mindless and as useless as paeons of chauvinistic praise.[9] To project an instant and perfect utopia, easily and perfectly achievable, is the mark of idealistic youth or of middle-aged muddle-headedness. A friend of mine used to say of college students that if they weren't socialists by 20 there was something wrong with them, and if they weren't over it by 30 there was something wrong with them.

The task before us is much more complicated, demanding, and permanent than our idealists or our revolutionaries realize.

The Prudent Response to Injustice: A Triple Defense

The Virtuous Man and Woman

The first and primary problem is the provision of more virtuous men and women. That sounds pollyannish; but it is absurd to think of developing a just society locally or across the planet without a dominant leadership of just men and women. In the early medieval theory of democratic decision making in case of divergence of opinion, the opinion of the "major et sanior pars" (the larger and more sensible group) was to be followed. This effort to combine quantitative democracy with intellectual and moral elitism foundered on practical difficulties. But the ideal of achieving democratic leadership of just and intelligent men is valid—indeed it is the only defense against a despair of society's future.[10]

Too many feel that we are caught in a ruthless, unstoppable machine; that nothing can be done to stop the future so inhumanly pictured by prophets and scholars. People ask desperately for a program: "What can I—What can we do?"

Unfortunately, the first step of the program is as essential as it is normally uninteresting and unexciting. I will put point 1 of my program of reforms in the words of E.F. Schumacher. After 297 pages of trenchant criticism and comment on current society and its structures, he concludes his book:

Everywhere people ask: "What can I actually *do*?" The answer is as simple as it is disconcerting: we can, each of us, work *to put our own inner house in order* [emphasis added]. The guidance we need for this work cannot be found in science or technology, the value of which utterly depends on the ends they serve; but it can still be found in the traditional wisdom of mankind.[11]

This was a ploy used already in the 16th century by Saint Francis Borgia. To a Spanish nobleman, lamenting the corruption of the age, he said, "I have a plan of reform. *I* will reform myself and then *you* reform yourself and so on." We must have a dominant leadership of virtuous, just men and women, of a *major et sanior pars*. Each person contributes *himself* first of all. There is no use talking of improvement and of a human future for the human race if each individual laments social injustice and yet in his own life conforms to the dominant sensate materialistic mores of current society.

Spiritual Awakening

The second point of my program: In order to stimulate individuals to a numerically vast and socially effective renewal, what needs to be done? Schumacher speaks of drawing on the "traditional wisdom" of the human race.

In view of his total book, I would judge that he means the "traditional religious and cultural wisdom of mankind." Here I find that Philip Sporn has expressed the second point of my proposed program better than I have been able to do. In a trenchant, dissenting note he says:

Surely, with so much trembling in the balance, we cannot permit ourselves to be overawed by technics, formulas, legalities, and diplomatic arrangements and leave assurance of man's survival on planet Earth entirely up to the governments of the world to provide . . . we need to appeal to and summon power and forces over and above government. We need to bring about a powerful revolution in man's dominant religious dedication to the life force and to form universally in a great moral life-saving movement to prevent the disappearance of life on earth.[12]

I speak of a just society. I think this comes to the same thing that Sporn refers to. We have reached a point where only a just society can survive. My second point, therefore, is to mount a worldwide religious movement to make individuals more spiritual, more virtuous, more just, so that they can effectively promote justice. We need an apolitical, worldwide coalition of religious leaders and groups, of Jews, Christians, Muslims, Buddhists,[13] Hindus, Confucianists to set up a crusade of the people to the people. It must be a totally apolitical crusade (this would currently be difficult for many Jews and Muslims); it must aim first of all at personal respiritualization (i.e., a total confrontation with sensate materialism in all its aspects) and as a religious movement only secondarily at the reform of unjust systems and structures. As religious leaders, while constantly representing the ideal of a just society and the basic principles essential thereto, those directing the crusade must hope to reform society primarily through the reform of individuals.

This second point in my program requires some recapitulation and some additional discussion. Aristotle pointed out that in an unjust state the "good" man (i.e., the virtuous or just man) is proportionately a "bad" citizen. We have already asserted and offered general indications that both our international and our national societies are, to varying extents, unjust societies. No good man therefore can wholly conform himself to existing institutions, structures, or societies.

On the other hand, the current structures are not entirely unjust and, except perhaps in a few cases, no net good will result from their total destruction. Add to this the idea born of sober reflection on either or both historical experience and Christian theology, that complete peace and justice are unattainable in historic humanity and will be present only in the eschatological Messianic kingdom. The just man must therefore accept[14] the unjust-just society as his working arena without personally conforming to it or totally approving. The Christian is always at least a bit uncomfortable in this world. The situation varies. The Christian in Russia, the Christian in Amin's Uganda, the Christian in the United States, all have to take different stances *vis-à-vis* their societies; the modes of abstention, of dissidence, and of material cooperation will vary greatly.

The Christian will always remain to some degree a civil and social dissident; if his Christianity is deep and active, he will be an active dissident. He need not and generally should not become a total adversary. At the other extreme the Christian who coalesces all his loyalties so as to identify with the status quo of a society or any social structure (such as a "Christian" political party) betrays himself, the Church, and society itself.[15]

Many Americans in the past almost identified their religion with their Americanism. For them, the increasing divergence between public policy and Christian morality has been shattering and has resulted in what Bellah calls the broken covenant.[16]

Recently Malachi Martin wrote in *The National Review* that, if the divergence between law and justice and morality in the United States should continue, Christians will have an opportunity, unprecedented in American history, to reassert and protect their religious beliefs in a manner approaching heroism and at least minor martyrdom.[17]

The Responsibilities of Universities and Churches

I now draw from these considerations conclusions concerning education, which constitutes the third point in my proposed program. It is clear that our schools and especially our universities must aim, among other things, at producing just men and women, especially just men and women capable of leadership. The kind of education needed must help men and women to develop not only modes of acting (i.e., training in the practice of justice by rote or rule), but also a personal possession of the virtue of justice.

The virtue of justice is the human, interior, self-possessed, consciously adopted determination to do the just thing combined with a comprehension of what the just thing is. One, there must be an intellectual component (supplied mainly by literature, philosophy, and theology) in which the total human situation is assessed and understood and in which basic ethical and humane principles are understood and accepted. Two, there must be an affective component which orients the will and all man's affective life toward the service of justice. Three, there must be a technical component to enable the graduates to participate effectively in some phase of social activity (law, business, politics, agriculture, religion) not only to keep it going productively, but to bring it into closer conformity with the demands of justice.[18]

The first of these requirements is primarily the concern of the liberal arts and sciences (with pride of place to philosophy and theology); the second is primarily the concern of campus ministry, student development, and personal counseling. The third is primarily the concern of specialized departments and schools. This division is to be understood as general, not as sharp and exclusive. Any good teacher will have an influence on the affective life of his students; technical specialities can be taught in a liberal and humanistic manner. Thus, all the components overlap and should be mutually reinforcing.

I am proposing a definite goal for higher education. I am quite aware that many colleges and universities have renounced any pretense of influencing the moral character of their students (and, in consequence, do effectively influence it for the worse). I am aware that departments of philosophy are no longer centers of high moral convictions and insights and that not all theologians can contribute to the goal I propose. Nonetheless, unless our churches and our schools undertake these goals, there is no hope. There are no other institutions that can stay the increasing sweep of injustice. The traditional mottoes of many of our institutions (*scientia et religio*; *bonis moribus et artibus*) should be given renewed meaning. Our religiously oriented institutions ought to lead the way.

The Necessity for Effective Dissidence

Finally, I want to re-emphasize several aspects of the matter. The education proposed should prepare persons who will indeed function within existing society but will not be totally conformed to it. It must be an education for nonconformity and for effective dissidence. The graduate will not be nicely adjusted to society; he should in fact feel uncomfortable in it. On the other hand, it should not aim at producing revolutionaries or incompetent do-gooders.[19]

The graduate can assume a productive and positive role in society, but he should do two things in addition. First, in all his personal relations, he should strive conscientiously to practice justice; thus, his own milieu and his own structure will be turned to justice. Second, he must work for reform of structures whenever it is sure to be needed. As an example: If indeed U.S. and British business structures do institutionalize greed (and therefore injustice), as E.F. Schumacher seems to think,[20] then these business structures should be changed or replaced. Schumacher himself suggests alternate types of corporate business structures.[21] Theodore V. Purcell, S.J. suggests the appointment of "corporate officers to be the corporation's ethical 'devil's advocate'—a sort of vice president in charge of ethics."[22] Activist groups have moved to interest shareholders in moral concern and to get public-minded members appointed to corporate boards. I cite these suggestions merely as examples of what I am advocating.

I want to emphasize my conviction that we must solve our problems through virtuous, intelligent, competent people. In response to the ethical crisis there has been a flurry of activity in setting up ethics committees, revised professional codes, and even new legislation. The American Institute of Certified

Public Accountants, the American Psychological Association, the American Bar Association, and many other groups have codes and are revising or reactivating them. These codes are useful guides, but they cannot solve the basic problem. Laws and regulations cannot be successful if they depend entirely on the policeman and the external punishments of associations and courts. No system will work unless those under it support it and to a large extent believe it is right and just.

So we are back to people. Without a *major et sanior pars* our society cannot survive. I reaffirm my conclusions: the family, the churches, and the educational institutions must return to their basic obligations to young men and women. They are the only institutions in our society that can restore the basic dedication to justice.

Notes

1. Cf. Josef Pieper, *Justice* (New York: Pantheon, 1955), pp. 34-39.
2. Quoted in Pieper, *Justice*, p. 50.
3. I am using "justice" in the broad philosophical sense. It includes but is not restricted to legal justice, civil rights, or quid-pro-quo arrangements.
4. Alfred Conard, *Corporations in Perspective* (Mineola, N.Y.: The Foundation Press, 1976), p. 147. See also U.S. Department of Commerce, Bureau of Census reports.
5. See Plutarch, *Banquet of the Seven Wise Men*, Chapter 11.
6. *Summa Theologicaie*, 2a2ae, 118, 1, ad 2.
7. Cf. E.F. Schumacher, *Small is Beautiful* (New York: Perennial Library, Harper & Row, 1975), pp. 163-190.
8. Recently a young girl was electrocuted in the bath tub when an electric curling device fell into the water.
9. For example, I believe that the Anglo-Saxon legal system has been perhaps the most equitable system of law ever devised by men. The "common law" has been called the only Christian system of law to survive the Middle Ages. I deliberately said that it "has been . . . equitable," because in recent years there have been disquieting indications that our legal system is losing its moral base, that our lawyers are less concerned with ethics and that our courts are arbitrarily moving beyond their charter. Nonetheless, our system has in the main promoted justice.
10. In a recent election I said our choice for president was between an idealistic fool and an intelligent crook. Democracy cannot survive a series of such choices.
11. Schumacher, *Small Is Beautiful*, p. 297.
12. Committee for Economic Development, *Nuclear Energy and National Security*, New York CED, 1976, p. 68.

13. Schumacher, *Small Is Beautiful*; see his interesting chapter on "Buddhist Economics," pp. 53-62.

14. Up to a point, of course.

15. At a time when city politics in Italy was played out as a see-saw between the Papal party (the Guelphs) and the Anti-Papal party (the Ghibellines), the following case of conscience was presented to Saint Thomas: "If a party wins control, exiles its opponents and seizes their property, is it bound to restitution?" Saint Thomas answered "Yes." But, the rejoinder went, what if the winning party was the party of the Church (the Guelphs)? Saint Thomas: "The *true* party of the Church is the one that practices justice; restitution is required."

16. Senator Albert J. Beveridge speaking before the United States Senate in January 1900 said: "And of all our race [i.e., the English speaking and Teutonic peoples] He [God] has marked the American people as His chosen nation to finally lead in the redemption of the world." Herman Melville wrote: "... almost for the first time in the history of the earth, national selfishness is unbounded philanthropy; for we cannot do a good to America, but we give alms to the world." Add to this the statement of a leading public figure that what is good for General Motors is good for America and we get the concatenation—what is good for General Motors is good for America, what is good for America is good for the world and its religious redemption. To abbreviate: What's good for General Motors is good for worldwide religion. These texts are quoted in: Robert N. Bellah, *The Broken Covenant* (New York: The Seabury Press, 1975), pp. 38-39.

17. Malachi Martin, "The Opportunity," *The National Review*, October 15, 1976, p. 1124.

18. In this sense higher education must produce people to serve and staff the system, since the welfare of all the people depends on the continuing function of existing structures. To close down the federal government (as the extreme activists planned to do in May of 1971 in Washington) or to shut down U.S. Steel would be a major disaster and a major injustice. No institution need apologize for preparing people to work in our industries, our professions, and our political life, provided that they balance this preparation with education for nonconformity and active promotion of change.

19. I am speaking mainly of the United States. A society may indeed reach such a level of injustice that violent action is the only recourse. I would say that Hitler's Germany had reached that point. The 16th century Jesuit theologian Mariana justified political assassination (tyrannicide) on individual judgment precisely on this ground. Obviously, this is an extreme and dangerous sort of decision and must meet a stiff set of moral criteria.

20. Cf. Schumacher, *Small Is Beautiful*, Part IV, Chapter 4.

21. Ibid., Chapter 5, pp. 272-292.

22. Theodore V. Purcell, S.J., "Institutionalizing Ethics into Top Management Decisions," A paper presented to the Association for Social Economics, Atlantic City, N.J., September 6, 1976.

Part III
The Individual and Society

Introduction to Part III

Inevitably, the individual business executive finds that his own moral code is the bottomline in business decision making. Is the individual executive caught in the middle of the moral dilemma? Does his success as a businessman clash with his responsibilities to society at large and to his own conscience? It is clear that the social environment of the business firm and the ethical standards of the individual executive who manages that firm are all bound up together.

There are two major schools of thought on crime and its control. One blames the criminals and advocates severe penalties for these criminal individuals. The other blames society for creating the conditions which "push" certain members of society to commit crimes. This latter school advocates, therefore, light penalties on the individual criminal and extensive efforts to improve society or eliminate the conditions which generate crime.

Similarly, in relation to unethical business actions, some blame both the business firm and the executive and thus advocate strong measures against them.[1] Others blame the competitive environment (arguments like "it is part of the business game") and therefore reject legislation to control business.

As Amitai Etzioni explains, the elected government sets the tone and example for moral conduct within society. Also, government effectively enforces compliance with majority rule by subjecting *individuals* (real people, not institutions, since the latter often take on characteristics of autonomy and nongovernability) who deviate from the rules to a range of punishments prescribed by society's legal code.

Only individual persons can be moral or immoral; business firms are not real persons, hence cannot be moral or immoral. Actions attributed to business firms are performed by individuals. It is these individuals who must be considered personally liable for whatever business firms are accused of doing. It is the individual executive who decides whether to act morally or immorally, ethically or unethically. This decision is based on his perception of a three-tiered value system, starting with society (its legal deterrents and moral leadership), then moving to the business firm (its attitude toward social responsibility leading to its moral climate) and finally to the individual himself (his own value system).

Business is not alone in its moral crisis. Max Lerner has pointed out that all the professions face a similar dilemma.[2] As illustrations of the dimensions of the problem, we include specific examples. Margaret Mead points up the moral environment of the scientific community and suggests that peer pressure through a science court can influence scientists to act professionally in accordance with societal goals. Sam Ervin, Jr., chairman of the Senate Watergate committee, examines the role of the lawyer in society and emphasizes the importance of law in determining values.

To lead businessmen through the maze of ethical decision making,

Yerachmiel Kugel and Gladys W. Gruenberg conclude the discussion with practical guidelines designed to allow each executive to tailor his decision to his own company and personal environment and values.

Notes

1. An example is the 1977 Senate bill against international payoffs, which levies a $500,000 fine against the business firm and a $10,000 fine and 5 years in jail against the individual executive. *The Wall Street Journal*, April 7, 1977.

2. Cf. Max Lerner, "The Shame of the Professions," *The Saturday Review*, November 1, 1975, pp. 10-12, reprinted in Kugel and Gruenberg, *Selected Readings on International Payoffs*.

7 Ethics and the Professions

7-1 Remarks Concerning the Science Court*

Margaret Mead

As I understand the issue that we have come to discuss, we are seeking ways in which scientific matters that are in doubt within the scientific community can be organized in a form that is useful to policymakers. The task force[1] has proposed a model drawn from the experience of the judiciary, involving the adversary system and a judicial panel, in the hope that the use of the adversary system would lead to a clarification of the disagreements within the scientific community. The task force has presented a fairly elaborate plan that includes the establishment of an Institute for Scientific Judgment—a science court mechanism which would select case managers from organizations bidding for the contracts, who would develop rules of procedure for conducting the discussion, evaluate the cogency of the advocates on each side, have the right of cross-examination, and deliver a judgment. The proposal is thus for a full-blown new institution which has been advocated since 1967.[2]

I propose to discuss this problem under the following headings:

1. The core aims of the proposal.
2. The advantages and disadvantages of the various components of the proposal.
3. The problem of establishing a new complete institution within U.S. society, and the alternatives that are open.
4. A suggestion as to next steps.

As I understand the aim of this proposal, it is to replace the present unsatisfactory way in which scientific evidence is marshalled for decision making by policymakers, and in which scientific disagreements are transmuted into ideological and special interest disagreements, so that conflicts of interest appear to be scientific because they are supported by scientists who are recruited because of genuine scientific disagreement. Even if there is no consideration of influencing the scientific witnesses through economic connections with the special interests involved—such as an industry, a government agency, a political

*Address at the Science Court Colloquium, U.S. Department of Commerce, September 20, 1976.

119

party—the way in which scientific evidence is introduced to prove a nonscientific case, that is, a case based on quite other considerations, is thoroughly unsatisfactory. Too often it turns into a debate, with victory going to the most eloquent and persuasive, something that the rules of scientific discourse are expressly designed to prevent.

So the problem becomes: How can an institution be created that can use the rules of scientific evidence and exclude the kinds of discussion that occur when there is a clash of interests? How can all other considerations be excluded, and the discussion conducted as it would be within the pages of a scientific journal, yet sharpened so that the issues of importance to the policymakers are directly addressed.

For example, in purely scientific discussion in such matters as to how soon a given pollution level may be reached or destruction of the ozone layer may occur, time is often unimportant. But to policymakers elected for short terms or subject to legislative whims, the time scale may be of the utmost importance. The chances of a danger five years hence, as compared with fifty years hence, take on enormous importance. Probabilities[3] assume very different proportionate importance when the calculations are being made by those who may be held responsible for disaster or may suffer directly from them.

Where scientific discourse attempts rigorously to exclude partisan emotion, many interpretive statements inevitably introduce it when scientists are asked to testify as expert witnesses. The emotion with which a scientific position is held is infused with the emotion which has centered about a policy issue, and the consequent result may obscure the scientific issues themselves.

The aim of the task force proposal is widely shared, namely, to purge discussions involving science of extraneous elements and organize it in such a way as to make it readily available for policymakers.

Evaluation of the Proposal

We then come to the proposal itself, which is modeled on a very ancient process—the judicial one—which has arisen from two sources: (1) the effort to determine the innocence or guilt of particular human beings so that they may be punished, and (2) the effort to arrive at an equitable solution, where two parties dispute as to what damage has been or is being done.

In the course of the development of the judicial process, the court or hearing place, with a judge or judges and jury of peers, the rules of presentation of evidence, and the adversary system allow each party to the dispute, whether it be state and individual accused or two civil litigants, to defend its position by every available means. As the system has developed, *justice* is not sought by either contestant, but there is a prevailing—although somewhat eroded—belief that justice will result from a process in which each side uses every method permitted to it, by the rules, to *win* the case for the client, to free the accused whether he is guilty or innocent, to get a settlement just or unjust favorable to the client. The possibility of appeal is used as a method of correcting errors in procedure.

Eloquence, drama, threats, special appeals to the prejudices of judge or jurors, in addition to the relative financial decisions, are all everyday factors in judicial decisions until the Supreme Court is reached, and there the composition of the court is admittedly of great importance. Not one of these procedures is congruent with the methods of science, where the aim in any scientific controversy is to resolve the controversy in the scientifically best way in terms of the existing paradigms in the field, to state the degree to which evidence is both good or inconclusive, and to ban eloquence, special pleading, partisan emotions from the whole proceeding. Any suggestion that a scientist has won a debate, rather than that his theoretical position has been fully supported by the scrutiny and replication of his results, suborns scientific work. We find such suborning occurring whenever a scientific issue becomes politicized by the introduction of politics within the scientific community.

Yet the fact remains that, when a scientific discussion is conducted within the pages of scientific journals and scientific meetings, it lacks the characteristics necessary for policymakers, who want to know something about the probability that one side or the other or several sides of an indecisive argument are *right*. It is only when there is genuine doubt that the arguments among scientists should be presented to policymakers at all. If the scientific results are currently clear and undisputed, policymakers have to take them into account and move to another level of discourse.

It would seem that, in addition to eliminating an unsatisfactory system of expert witnesses vying with each other in eloquence and plausibility in ways wholly inappropriate to scientific discussions, what is needed is a way to make the genuine scientific uncertainties clear and relevant. Unless the disagreeing scientists are forced to be relevant, they may present a large number of peripheral quibbles, which can be seized upon and exploited by political partisans of some policy.

Thus we may ask, what is there in our entire judicial procedure that throws light on how to obtain clarity and relevance? In the first place, translation is required within a court proceeding whenever a witness uses another language, and court proceedings may be halted until an adequate interpreter is found. This requirement could be applied to all scientific "hearings," and translation satisfactory to those who will have to make the final decision on policy should be insisted upon, just as evidence couched in a foreign language has to be translated in any proper court.

Relevance, the second requirement, also has to be forced, or the proponents of different scientific positions may choose to phrase the discussion in ways that may be more scientifically congenial, but which do not relate to those things the decision makers need to know. Here the judicial pattern of cross-examination, that highlights neglected aspects of the discussion and forces a review of the data and insists upon statements of proportionate importance, could be facilitative.

Whether the cross-examination should be conducted by the scientific witnesses themselves or should become a special profession is I believe, one of the important decisions to be made as we consider which aspects of this science court should be adopted. Obviously, in any preliminary pilot or feasibility study, there would be no professional scientific cross-examiners in existence, as there would eventually be if an adversary system in its entirety were to be adopted.

Perhaps more important than forcing the scientific witnesses to be intelligible and to concentrate on the issues relevant to policy, is the need to exclude irrelevance, red herrings artfully constructed to obscure the point, that would certainly be involved if sides or parties to a disputed scientific point were retained or funded by any kind of interest group.

In a court an advocate may appeal against the introduction of extraneous evidence. In a science court mechanism such as the one being envisioned here, there is a question as to whose responsibility it would be to insist upon the exclusion of irrelevant material. Within a full adversary system the matter is left to the clash between the advocates to be ruled on by the judge. In a scientific meeting the chairman may, if he is sufficiently courageous, play that role. A satisfactory mechanism for obtaining the desired clarity, intelligibility and relevance within this proposed institutional framework is obviously central to the whole problem.

When the institution of a court is used as the model, the question of the judge or panel of judges or jury rendering a verdict or decision immediately arises. The present proposal envisions a panel which would give decisions. But when scientific evidence and scientific opinion are at variance with one another, *there can be no decision.* If there were a possible decision, scientists would agree and a very different kind of witness would be needed.

If scientists agree, the burden on the decision makers is whether to prefer political or economic reasons to scientific statements, relating to such matters as the hazards to human well-being or the destruction of the environment. The decision makers may well say that they think considerations of national defense or immediate full employment or even the continuation in power of the political party override all scientific evidence. But they cannot cite scientific evidence on both sides of the question.

It could perhaps be that with a science court mechanism the scientists, when forced to be intelligible, policy oriented, and relevant, might find that there was no relevant scientific disagreement; the kind of evidence presented to the policymakers would therefore be of a different kind. Probing the amount of disagreement among scientists and attempting to find some common ground of relevant agreement might be one of the functions of the science court mechanism which is under discussion here. But this would not be a verdict or decision of a judge; it would be a consensus among the different scientific witnesses, after they had been subjected to the procedures which forced them to be relevant.[a]

It is possible that if there were an efficient mechanism of this sort, one of the most troublesome questions for policymakers—the exclusion of the scientists who know most about the subject at issue because of conflicts of interest— would be resolved. If there were rigorous scientific cross-examination, such experts could be admitted to the proceedings. (The pharmaceutical industry is a good example of present difficulty with qualified witnesses and the fact that there is no appeal from an FDA decision.)

Furthermore, since "research" has become a big industry[5] with very large sums and large amounts of power at stake, the concomitants of such conditions have been emerging steadily—special pleading within the community of scientists.

Proposed Institutional Form

So far, I have considered the proposal in terms of process and its appropriateness or inappropriateness to resolve scientific disagreements. I would now like to turn to the question of the proposed institutional form and its various components. The proposal includes a profession of *case managers*, contracts from organizations who would bid for them, retaining or funding from ideologically opposed interest groups, e.g., the Atomic Industrial Forum and the Sierra Club, and the enlistment of highly trained scientific specialists as a panel of judges who would render a decision. The case managers would each be expected to "present the best case," that is, to try to win for their sides.

The question is left open as to the level of such courts, whether there would be a Science Court at the national level, which is certainly the way that the opponents of the idea have interpreted it, or whether there would be a mechanism called a science court which could be used at the state and local levels—a pattern of behavior rather than an identified institution located in one place. Most of the criticism has been leveled at the idea of *A Science Court*, localized in Washington, D.C., and financed by the federal government, which would render verdicts. Almost all objections that I have raised apply to the court model. A verdict, the adversary system, the idea that there could be judges who could give a verdict, all in *a priori*, the notion that the interest groups would finance the presentation of scientific evidence for their partisan advocacy—these are all incompatible with scientific discourse and the methods of science.

However, the idea of a *new mechanism*, which would supersede the present system of expert witnesses and provide a method by which scientific uncertain-

---

[a]I recently participated in an attempt to produce such a consensus among atmospheric scientists that failed; the only consensus they reached was on the need for more research![4]

ties could be rendered intelligible and relevant to policymakers, is an important goal. In the task force's contemplated pattern, an Institute of Scientific Procedures responsible for elaborating and monitoring could be used, probably with varying degrees of success and expertise at different governmental levels. In the development of such a process we have, if we consider the history of institutional innovations in the United States, different options.[6]

The institute could undertake to train and provide specialists in the process so that, if the city of Fall River or the State of Idaho wishes to use the mechanism, experts could be supplied, which would assure that the process was correctly carried out. The use of the mechanism, once it was well enough established, could be mandated just as an autopsy can be mandated, with the requirement that the practitioner who performs the autopsy be certified, or an audit could be mandated and the competency of the process be certified, as schools and standards for certified public accountants are maintained. The specialized practitioners would have competency in certain legal practices which are being used as models—cross-examination, exclusion of irrelevant and immaterial evidence, etc.—and competency in certain fields of science. Thus, both a mechanism that could be mandated and a profession that could carry out the mechanism in a reasonably standard and responsible way could be developed.

Alternatively, the idea could be propagated without the safeguards of institutional control over training and practice. When an idea is propagated in U.S. society, it is very rapidly altered, often diluted, distorted, and prostituted, although it does not necessarily lose all efficacy. Hearings are an example; the word *hearing* carries an aura of fairness, of openness, of a belief that some group who has the power to act is giving a fair chance to both or several sides of an argument. In practice, hearings can be totally packed and maneuvered, or open and likely to lead to better decisions. There is no institution that can decide whether hearings are open or shut, packed or fair, and yet the fact that there were hearings can be used to justify a legislative or administrative action, to reject criticism, and very often to stifle legitimate public discussion. There are many instances of brilliant inventions and brilliant additions to inventions, as when Robert Lamb extended the hearings of the Tollen Commission over the country so that hearings were held where problems of migratory labor were actually salient.[7] But there are also a great many instances of the dilution and perversion of such inventions.

Panels at public meetings were invented to give the different constituencies in a large audience a voice as the loudspeaker system increased the dominance of the podium over the floor, and to prevent the fortuitousness of an unsystematic choice from those who reach the microphone on the floor first. Today a panel can be any group of more than two persons, and is often used just to increase the appeal of a meeting by including more well known people. It can be used for the original purpose, but there is no way of assuring that it will be.

The same thing is true of a number of institutional inventions like group dynamics, indirect interviewing, group therapy, various "anonymous" groups. The idea diffuses, and there is no control over form or practitioner so that much of its usefulness is lost. The same kind of distortion occurs within the scientific community; ideas like *peer refereeing* for projected proposals or scientific articles can be abused;[8] attempts to attain honesty by promising confidentiality are replaced by demands that the referee's opinion be public, thus sacrificing real evaluation to an appearance of fairness.[9] There is no guarantee that even an institution which maintained control over training and procedure could not be subverted. But past history suggests that such controls might ensure a much greater usefulness.

Next Steps

Finally, I would like to discuss next steps. The proposal speaks of an experiment, using the word *experiment* in its popular form to mean trying out something that may not work. I think it is undesirable—in a scientific context—to use the term this way. *Pilot* or *feasibility study* would be preferable. Pilot hearings embodying one or more features of the plan could be inaugurated, or monitored when carried out by other organizations.

Records could be analyzed of recent events such as the confrontation demanded by the Atomic Industrial Forum before the National Council of Churches,[10] in which scientific witnesses produced by both sides and a panel of ethicists were convened who rendered verdicts in terms of the cogency of the arguments—not the data. The Scientists Institute for Public Information recently held a meeting on the economic viability of nuclear energy, for the members of Congress and their staffs cosponsored with the Environmental Study Conference on June 7, 1976, in which cross-examination was a principal feature. The National Academy of Sciences held hearings in regard to a committee mandate on nuclear and alternate energy systems on January 22, 1976.

Analysis of a set of these events in which one or more of the proposed techniques have been used could be made by a small group of lawyers and social scientists versed in the analysis of institutions. Questions like the proposal of environmental groups on one side and industry groups on the other could be examined with the financial and ethical implications in comparison with other models, such as industries on both sides, labor unions on both sides, and environmental groups on both sides, to point up the complexity of the interest groups who would be concerned if an adversary system were adopted. A small group of able potential practitioners could be assembled and given crash training, and their services volunteered in relatively small and limited disputes.

A variety of trials of feasibility would seem desirable, especially in the light of the establishment of the President's Advisory Committee on Science, Engineering and Technology by the White House on May 9, 1976, with its one year mandate. Such pilot and feasibility studies could very well feed into that committee rather than into a full-blown institution appearing as a rival to its recommendations.

A study should be made of the present associations with the idea of a court in the minds of U.S. voters.[11] I think we would find that the word is associated with a place where justice or injustice is done dependent on whether those involved are poor or rich and influential, and that there is very little association with the word *truth*. We know that the responses to the words *science* and *scientist* are very mixed.[12] The kind of public acceptance that might come from joining the word *court* to the word *science* might mobilize exceedingly negative feelings.

In closing, I emphasize that some mechanism such as the task force proposes is very much needed, and we should be indebted to them for persistence in advocating it. I have been interested in the idea since it was first proposed in 1967, and began examination of the relative merits of the adversary system, the expert witness, and the brief of a friend of the court, in their appropriateness and efficacy.

Notes

1. Task Force of the Presidential Advisory Group on Anticipated Advances in Science and Technology, "The Science Court Experiment: An Interim Report," *Science*, August 20, 1976, pp. 653-656. Kantrowitz, Arthur, "Controlling Technology Democratically," *American Scientist* (September-October, 1975, pp. 505-509.

2. Kantrowitz, Arthur, testimony before United States Senate, Subcommittee on Government Research, Committee on Government Operations, March 16, 1967. *Congressional Record*, June 8, 1967, p. 15256. Kantrowitz, Arthur, "Proposal for an Institution for Scientific Judgment," *Science*, May 12, 1967, pp. 763-764.

3. Lee, Kai N., Review of *Acceptable Risk* by William W. Lowrance (Los Altos: Kaufmann, 1976). *Science*, July 9, 1976, pp. 138-139. Calabresi, Guido, "Reflections on Medical Experimentation in Humans," *Daedalus*, Spring, 1969, pp. 387-405.

4. Mead, Margaret, and Kellogg, William, eds., *The Atmosphere: Endangered and Endangering*, conference sponsored by The John E. Fogarty International Center and The National Institute of Environmental Health Sciences, October 1975.

5. Committee on the Social Sciences, National Science Foundation, Assembly of Behavioral and Social Sciences, National Research Council, *Social and Behavioral Science Programs in the National Science Foundation*. Washington, D.C.: National Academy of Sciences, 1976. Mead, Margaret, "Statement,

National Science Foundation Authorization Legislation, 1976." United States Senate, Special Subcommittee on the National Science Foundation, Committee on Labor and Public Welfare, *Hearings* on S.3202, March 1 and 3, 1976. Washington, D.C., 1976, pp. 192-197.

6. Mead, Margaret, *Continuities in Cultural Evolution* (New Haven: Yale University Press, 1964). Mead, Margaret and Byers, Paul, *The Small Conference: An Innovation in Communication* (Paris and The Hague: Mouton, 1968).

7. Mead, Margaret, "Robert K. Lamb: 1904-1952," *Human Organization* (May 1954), pp. 33-37.

8. Medawar, P.B., "The Strange Case of the Spotted Mice," a review of *The Patchwork Mouse*, by Joseph Hixson. *The New York Review*, April 15, 1976, pp. 6-11.

9. Rynkiewich, Michael A. and Spradley, James P., *Ethics and Anthropology: Dilemmas in Fieldwork.* (New York: John Wiley, 1976).

10. *A Consultation on the Plutonium Economy*, sponsored by the Division of Church and Society, National Council of Churches, Riverside Church, New York, January 28, 1976.

11. Levine, Maurice, *Psychiatry and Ethics* (New York: George Braziller, 1972).

12. Mead, Margaret and Metraux, Rhoda, "Image of the Scientist among High-School Students," *Science*, August 30, 1957, pp. 384-390.

7-2 The Role of the Lawyer in America*

Sam J. Ervin, Jr.

It is our proud boast as Americans that our national and state constitutions were ordained to establish for our people governments of laws instead of governments of men; and it is my purpose to demonstrate that these governments of laws cannot operate effectively for the benefit of our people without the assistance of the lawyer.

Sir Thomas More envisioned his imaginary nation, Utopia, as a land in which justice was administered without laws and without lawyers. The unreality of Sir Thomas' vision is manifest. Justice cannot exist anywhere without lawyers to champion it and laws to enforce it.

It is obvious, moreover, that the Republic which the Founding Fathers gave to America will vanish if America ceases to have a government of laws. Alexander Hamilton, who was a brilliant lawyer, explained why this is so. He said:

---
*From a speech delivered at the sixth annual Law Day dinner held by New England School of Law on May 1, 1975. Reprinted with permission from *New England Law Review* (Fall 1975), pp. 1-6. All rights reserved by Senator Ervin.

> It has been frequently remarked with great propriety that a voluminous code of laws is one of the inconveniences necessarily connected with advantages of a free government.[1]

In saying this, Hamilton emphasized that a government of laws necessarily requires many laws to define and limit the powers of government and its officers and many laws to elaborate the rights and the responsibilities of the people.

At the same time he warned his contemporaries and subsequent generations of Americans that "the facility and excess of law-making seem to be the diseases to which our governments are most liable";[2] that "all the repealing, explaining, and amending laws, which fill and disgrace our voluminous codes (are) but so many monuments of deficient wisdom";[3] and that the incessant multiplying and altering of laws will produce disastrous consequences.

He described these consequences in these words:

> The internal effects of a mutable policy are still more calamitous. It poisons the blessings of liberty itself. It will be of little avail to the people if the laws are made by men of their own choice, if the laws be so voluminous that they cannot be read, or so incoherent that they cannot be understood; if they be repealed or revised before they are promulgated, or undergo such incessant changes that no man who knows what the law is today can guess what it will be tomorrow. Law is defined to be a rule of action; but how can that be a rule, which is little known and less fixed?[4]

Our laws have multiplied a thousand-fold since Alexander Hamilton's day. Many of them have been the inevitable results of the increasing complexities of society. But many of them, I believe, are unnecessary and harmful products of a mania which has harassed our land in recent years.

Whenever anything they deem undesirable from their particular points of view happens, some politically powerful groups of Americans cry out for the immediate enactment of new laws. Their legislators, federal and state, hastily respond by passing new laws, often without pausing to determine whether the remedy for the supposed evil must be found in ethics or religion rather than in law, or whether the old laws are adequate to cope with the supposed evil, or whether the new laws are designed to deal with the supposed evil in a just and rational way.

What has been said makes America's need for competent lawyers plain. After all, the laws prescribe rules of conduct for all public officials and private individuals in our land. These officials and individuals are bound at their peril to observe these rules of conduct, even though they may not know or understand the laws which prescribe them. This is so because a government of laws would collapse if ignorance of law were an accepted excuse for its violation.

These public officials and private individuals require the services of competent lawyers to counsel them in respect to the legality of the actions they may contemplate taking in the future, or to act as their advocate in respect to actions which they or others may have taken in the past.

What I have just said reveals in simple words the role of the lawyer in America. In executing his role, the lawyer engages in activities incident to the practice of law. He may advise his client in respect to his legal rights or responsibilities, or draft the legal documents necessitated by his client's personal or business affairs, or act as agent for his client in negotiating and consummating commercial transactions with others, or act as an advocate for his client in legal proceedings before courts or administrative tribunals. In doing any of these things, the lawyer owes his client complete and dedicated allegiance.

To protect prospective clients and the public against incompetent or unscrupulous lawyers, government requires every applicant for admission to the bar to demonstrate in appropriate ways that he has a fair knowledge of law and a trustworthy character. Moreover, it disbars from further practice lawyers who show themselves unworthy of possessing a law license by violating specified laws or ethical standards.

A lawyer performs his role in an acceptable manner if he discharges with reasonable skill and with fidelity the obligations which his high calling imposes upon its practitioners. These obligations consist of his obligation to his client, his obligation to the court or administrative tribunal before which he appears, his obligation to society, and his obligation to himself. I will endeavor to delineate these obligations.

The lawyer is not obliged to accept as a client anyone who seeks his professional aid. But whenever he undertakes to perform any legal task for a client, he impliedly assures his client that he possesses reasonable legal knowledge and skill; that he is competent or will make himself competent in apt time by study of the relevant facts and law to perform his undertaking in reasonable fashion; and that in performing his undertaking he will exercise his knowledge and skill with diligence and fidelity solely in his client's interest.

If his undertaking requires him to act as an advocate for his client, he impliedly gives the additional assurance to his client that he is reasonably acquainted with the rules of practice of the court or administrative tribunal before which he is to appear. But he does not undertake that the client will prevail in his cause, or profess that he knows all the law, or is incapable of error or mistake in applying it to the facts. As the Supreme Court remarked on one occasion, even the most skillful of the profession would hardly be able to come up to that high standard.[5]

The lawyer also owes to his client the duty to maintain inviolate his confidences and secrets, and to be intellectually honest in all dealings with him.

I cannot overmagnify the crucial importance of accuracy and diligence on the part of the lawyer. As Daniel Webster so well said:

Accuracy and diligence are more necessary to a lawyer than great comprehension of mind, or brilliancy of talent. . . . If he would be a great lawyer, he must first consent to become a great drudge.

Some laymen criticize lawyers for defending persons the laymen believe guilty of the offenses charged. When criticized for appearing for an unworthy client, Phocion, a lawyer of ancient Greece, replied that "the good have no need of an advocate."[6] Accused persons, who are deemed guilty or hated by the public, stand in greatest need of an advocate because it may be that they are innocent.

It is not the function of the lawyer to determine the guilt of persons charged with criminal offenses. Besides, no person is guilty in law until he has confessed his guilt or been convicted in open court. Hence, legal ethics adjudges rightly that "a lawyer has a right to defend a person accused of crime regardless of his personal opinion as to guilt. He is bound by all fair and honorable means to present every available defense to uphold due process of law."[7]

Justice Story and Thomas Erskine, the eminent English advocate, made significant remarks on this subject. I quote them:

Justice Story: He (the lawyer) may be required to defend against the arm of the government a party standing charged with some odious crime, real or imaginary. He is not at liberty to desert even the guilty wretch in his lowest estate; but he is bound to take care, that even here the law shall not be bent or broken to bring him to punishment. He will, at such times, from love of the law, as well as from compassion, freely give of his talents to the cause, and never surrender the victim until the judgment of his peers has convicted him upon legal evidence.[8]

Thomas Erskine: If the advocate refuses to defend from what he may think of the charge or of the defense, he assumes the character of the judge; nay, he assumes it before the hour of judgment; and in proportion to his rank or reputation, puts the heavy influence of, perhaps, a mistaken opinion into the scale against the accused.[9]

The client retains the lawyer's talents, but not his conscience. Hence a lawyer is never justified in doing an illegal or unethical act to serve a client.

The law entrusts to the lawyer an indispensable part in the operation of our adversary system of justice. As a consequence, it imposes upon him an obligation to aid courts and administrative tribunals in their efforts to make that system work in a way which accomplishes its objective and inspires confidence in the public. To this end, he must display respect for courts and administrative tribunals, defend them against unjust criticism, and act with decorum and dignity in his appearances before them. Moreover, he must exercise diligence in preparing the cause of his client for presentation to the court or administrative tribunal, and present the facts and the law relevant to the cause of his client at the hearing before the court or administrative tribunal with fairness and candor.

A lawyer demeans himself and trifles with a court or administrative tribunal if he takes a position before it which is not worthy of serious notice. But he is justified in taking a position based on law or a cogent argument that the law on which his adversary relies is unjust and ought to be modified or reversed. A lawyer does a grave disservice to his client and to the cause of justice itself if he accepts a retainer to try a case which he is too busy or too lazy to prepare for trial.

Society gives much to the lawyer. By prescribing for him arduous studies to fit him for admission to the bar, by granting to him authority to act as legal adviser, draftsman, and agent to others in connection with their personal and business affairs, and by committing to him the performance of an essential part in the administration of justice, society enables the lawyer to acquire a special competence in respect to many of its most important concerns.

As a consequence, society rightly expects that the lawyer will use his special competence to insure good government,to improve law and its administration, to promote the trust of the people in the legal profession and the administration of justice, to rid the legal profession of unworthy members, to make legal assistance available to the indigent, to defend hated individuals and unpopular causes in criminal proceedings, and to act in other respects as an upright, patriotic citizen.

The obligation of the lawyer to himself is to cherish and keep inviolate in all his professional activities that priceless element of good character, which we call integrity. The famous theologian, Cotton Mather, had this obligation in mind when he admonished the lawyers of Massachusetts in 1710 "to keep constantly a court of chancery in your own breast."[10]

I have observed lawyers at work ever since that far distant day in August, 1919, when the Supreme Court of North Carolina granted me a license to practice law. I rejoice to bear witness in closing that with rare exceptions they have performed in commendable fashion their obligations to clients, courts, administrative tribunals, society and themselves.

Notes

    1. *The Federalist* No. 78, at 495-496 (B.F. Wright ed. 1961) (A. Hamilton).

    2. Id.

    3. Id.

    4. *The Federalist* No. 62, at 411-412 (B.F. Wright ed. 1961) (A. Hamilton).

    5. National Savings Bank v. Ward, 100 U.S. 195 (1879); see also Lord Chief Justice Tindal in Lanphier v. Phipos, 8 C. & P. 475 (1838).

    6. *Plutarch's Lives.*

    7. R.L. Wise, *Legal Ethics* 320 (2d ed. 1970).

    8. J. Story, *Miscellaneous Writings* 521 (1852).

    9. Stryker, *For the Defense* 217 (1949); Thomas Erskine (Lord Erskine) on the trial of Thomas Paine for publishing *The Rights of Man*, 1792.

    10. C. Mather, *Bonifacius* 127 (1966).

8 Conclusion: Ethical Guidelines for Decision Making

Yerachmiel Kugel and
Gladys W. Gruenberg

Now that we have explored the nature and rationale of ethical business conduct, it is time to come closer to the bottomline and provide criteria for the determination of the conditions under which the individual executive should or should not act ethically. The main focus of this dilemma is the conflict between what is proper (ethics) and what is profitable (economics). The emphasis has been on the importance of individual rather than business accountability for the rewards or penalties pertaining to ethical or unethical decisions.

The criteria and guidelines for decision making are therefore individually oriented. There are four distinct steps to be taken by the executive before a final decision whether or not to act ethically can be made. These steps are depicted in the decision-making tree in figure 8-1.

Step 1. In the first step the executive determines whether the action he is considering is legal. If it is clearly within the white area of ethical conduct and presents no problem of legality, the executive has no dilemma on taking the action. If, on the other hand, the executive has reservations about the legality of the action (i.e., it is in the gray or black area), then he must move to the next step of the model.

Step 2. Once the conflict between economics and ethics has been joined, it behooves the executive to consider the matter in the context of the company's moral climate. Thus, the second step of the model deals with the moral climate of the company which constrains the individual executive. If that moral climate does not permit the action classified in the gray or black area, the executive's decision must be to refuse the action, and no further consideration of the matter is required. If, on the other hand, the company moral climate is ambivalent enough to permit the action, the executive should move to the next step of the model.

Step 3. The third step of the model deals with the economic considerations of the action. These include costs of legal counsel, the costs and benefits involving the company's public image, and the expected direct and indirect costs and benefits to be derived from the proposed action. If the benefits do not outweigh the costs, the action should be refused. If, on the other hand, the benefits outweigh the costs, then from the company's standpoint, the action should be taken. However, there is still a final step.

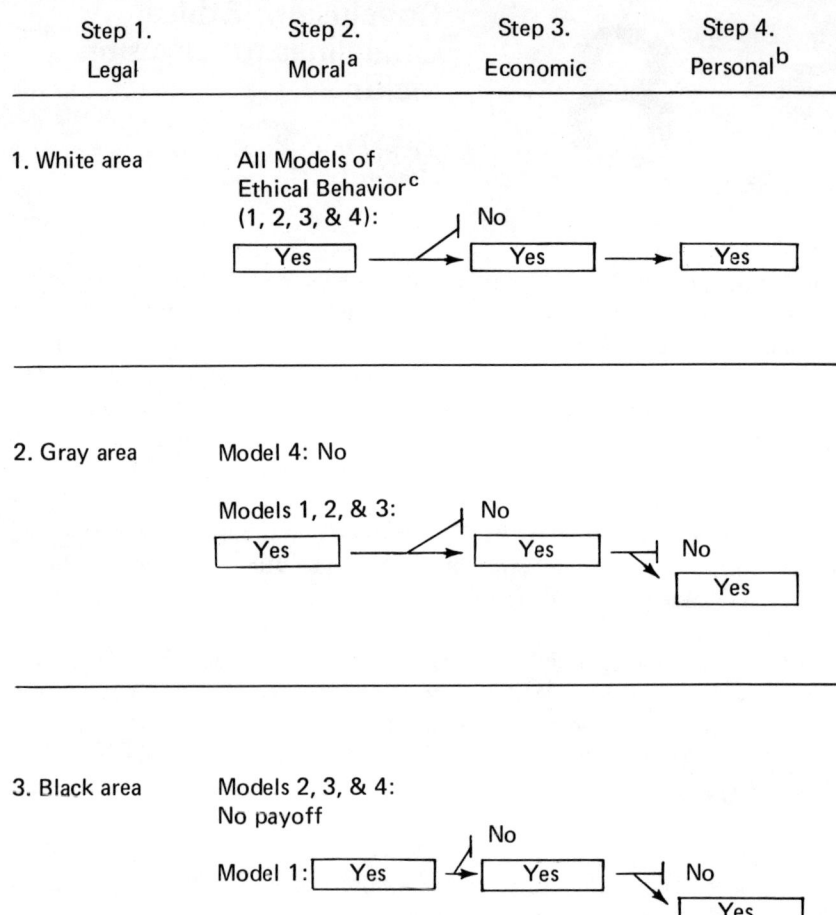

Source: Adapted from model appearing in Yerachmiel Kugel and Gladys W. Gruenberg, *International Payoffs: Dilemma for Business* (Lexington, Mass.: Lexington Books, D.C. Heath and Company, 1977), chapter 6.

[a]Business can be characterized by the following moral climate: *Model 1*–No moral consideration, *Model 2*–No moral consideration unless penalty, *Model 3*– Moral only for P-R purposes, *Model 4*–Morality in toto. Selection of ethical models must be oriented toward future (short and long run) rather than past.

[b]Individuals, although influenced by institutional moral leadership or climate, determine institutional morality not vice versa. Before they decide whether to act unethically, they must consider both personal economic and non-economic factors that bear on such a decision. For comparison of ethical models for other professions, see table 1-1.

[c]For detailed description of models, see table 1-1.

Figure 8-1. Decision-Making Model for Ethical Action.

Step 4. Individuals are responsible for company decisions; therefore, their own personal cost-benefit and moral calculations must be made before a decision on whether or not a specific action should be taken. Thus, the final step of the model deals with the personal considerations involved in taking the action.

To reinforce the types of considerations which the executive encounters as he gets involved in the decision-making process, refer to the article "Is Ethics Good Business?" and table 4-1, that sets forth the specific questions that must be answered to arrive at the final cost-benefit calculation.

About the Editors

Yerachmiel Kugel is professor of management sciences at Saint Louis University, where he also serves as associate director of the International Business Program. Since receiving the Ph.D. from Michigan State University, he has published numerous articles in professional and technical journals relative to multinational business behavior and serves as consultant to many organizations engaged in transnational operations.

Together with Dr. Gruenberg, Dr. Kugel is coauthor of *International Payoffs: Dilemma for Business* (Lexington Books, 1977) and is coeditor of *Selected Readings on International Payoffs* (Lexington Books, 1977). He is currently under contract with Oceana publications to write a book and to provide an annual update on the subject of legislation relative to business ethics throughout the world.

Gladys W. Gruenberg is professor of economics at Saint Louis University. In addition to courses in economic theory and policy, she teaches business ethics and comparative labor markets. As an arbitrator and accredited personnel diplomate she is interested in the impact of economic policies on human resources both in the United States and abroad.

Professor Gruenberg is associate director of the Personnel and Industrial Relations Program at the School of Business and Administration and is a past chapter president of the Industrial Relations Research Association. She is a member of the American and Southern Economic Associations and of the Association for Social Economics.